WASHING

DISHES

IS GOOD

FOR YOU

dept.store *for* the mind

WASHING

DISHES

IS GOOD

FOR YOU

MINDFUL LIVING IN
THE DAILY GRIND

aster

A Hachette UK Company

www.hachette.co.uk

First published in Great Britain in 2017 by Aster, a division of
Octopus Publishing Group Ltd, Carmelite House
50 Victoria Embankment, London EC4Y 0DZ
www.octopusbooks.co.uk
www.octopusbooksusa.com

Distributed in the US by Hachette Book Group
1290 Avenue of the Americas
4th and 5th Floors, New York, NY 10104

Distributed in Canada by Canadian Manda Group
664 Annette St., Toronto, Ontario, Canada M6S 2C8

ISBN 978-1-91202-316-5

A CIP catalog record for this book is available from the British Library.

Printed and bound in China

10 9 8 7 6 5 4 3 2 1

Consultant publisher Kate Adams
Senior Editor Pauline Bache
Copy Editor Alison Wormleighton
Consultant Editor Ruth Williams
Senior designer Jaz Bahra for Octopus
Creative direction and design Katie Steel and Jo Raynsford at Supafrank
Illustrator Veronica Wood
Photography James Champion
Production Manager Caroline Alberti

dept.store *for* the mind

BEAUTIFUL WORDS FOR THE MIND

Each book offers stories and ideas about creating daily habits that are kind
to the mind, whether through our connection with nature, our creativity, or
everyday tasks, or simply knowing and feeling more accepting of ourselves.
The books stretch the mind and soul, so that we may color outside of the lines,
experience the moments of wonder that are right there in front of us,
and occasionally venture out of our safe harbors.

deptstoreforthemind.com is the exciting new creative venture by Sophie
Howarth, cofounder of the School of Life. The Department Store for the Mind
is a place to explore the world inside your head: a vast and unique terrain of
thoughts, ideas, emotions, and memories.

www.deptstoreforthemind.com

INTRODUCTION

Can doing the dishes really be good for you? Can we discover a moment of insight, a wave of calm, a tickle of delight, or a tingle of connection within our simple, readily available, everyday routine? Without needing to alter our entire lifestyle, can we unearth a fresh way in, hidden inside the daily and seemingly mundane? How might we flip our thinking away from resisting and toward maybe even relishing doing the dishes, the cleaning, and the cooking? What might this do for our body, our mind, and our relationships?

One everyday activity at a time, artists, designers, writers, psychologists, and speakers share their stories and experiences of the everyday. You will hear of family bonding while doing the dishes, wondrous rituals with a cup of tea, and the creation of playful households.

Each chapter invites you to witness a personal journey and take from it what you will. In a world where so much of the noise around us suggests we are not good enough as we are, and that we must seek to change, these accounts try to do something different. They aim instead to invite a stroll into the complex pathways of the mind to discover the beauty of our own quirky individuality.

As we get more adept at feeling good about our own funny ways, we may become more able to warm to the same in others. Through tending ourselves, we may go some way to tending our world.

So, yes, we are suggesting that doing the dishes can be good for you. In fact, even more than good for you! It can be liberating, relaxing, creative, and healing. These ideas are deeply embedded in some of the world's most ancient wisdom. Here, we simply explore how this way of thinking can very easily become part of our daily doing.

At the close of each chapter you will discover suggestions and ideas about how to create simple daily habits from the writer's thinking. Some ideas might work for you and others will pass you by. This is perfectly fine as there are enough for each reader to discover a little gem to make their own.

WHAT'S ON YOUR PLATE?

CHAPTER 1

CHAPTER 1

WHAT'S ON YOUR PLATE?

My life doing the dishes

Meredith Whitely | Food at Heart

"When you are washing up, you should just be washing up."

The sentence ran through my mind as I dipped my kitchen knives into the hot, soapy water.

I'd just been reading *The Miracle of Mindfulness* by Thich Nhat Hanh. I don't read that many books written specifically about mindfulness (I'm normally too busy pawing through my cookbooks and magazines), but this is a short, beautiful book filled with simple stories and meditation practices. However, it turns out that some of the simplest things, like being fully present while doing the dishes, are also the most difficult.

When I'm standing at the sink, I could be planning for the weekend, composing an email in my head, thinking about what I'm eating for breakfast tomorrow, or even a recipe I need to write.... The list goes on.

When I'm doing the dishes, how often do I focus on doing the dishes? On honest contemplation, it turns out to be not so much.

Even in our modern dishwasher world, most days contain at least a little dishwashing by hand, even if it's just to rinse out a mug for a cup of coffee. But this is normally en route to some other activity or event, or a household hassle to get out of the way. This everyday act passes through our lives, often without our noticing.

12

" "

WHEN I'M DOING THE DISHES, HOW OFTEN DO I FOCUS ON DOING THE DISHES?

On reflecting some more, it surprised me to recognize that doing the dishes has been a tool of learning from the time I was a small child. Looking back, I can see what the time around the sink has taught me, and how it has played a part in guiding me toward who I am and what I do today.

DISHWASHING TOWARD TEAMWORK

I come from a family of food lovers who sat together every night for the evening meal. As with many large families, we were and are a noisy family. The kitchen table was a chance for us to talk, share, debate, and, occasionally when I was a sullen teenager, sulk. The easy flow of "talking over each other" dinner conversation was a connective tissue.

The talk was punctuated by delicious food created by my mother. She is an exceptionally talented cook, and, growing up in the abundant climes of Perth in Western Australia, we had access to a myriad of wonderful ingredients to enjoy. The only slight problem was that in a family of five children, this meant a lot of dishes to do at the end of a meal. My mother, an ultra-organized primary school teacher and avowed dishwasher-rejecter, dealt with this in a very practical way: by designing a dishwashing roster.

We were each assigned the role of washer, dryer, or put-away-er, and would rotate the role each night. This was written on a chart to avoid any confusion or arguments. Any thoughts of rebellion were futile—plus the threat of a docked allowance was a stick big enough to keep us in check. It was also unknowingly one of my earliest lessons in teamwork.

My brothers were much younger than the three girls, so we were initially a merry girl band of dishwashers. (I'm the middle child in case you're wondering.) My favorite task of the three was putting the dishes away. There was something about the stacking and orderliness that I still enjoy today. My eldest sister, on the other hand, could see the benefit of the washing part as it meant you'd be done and dusted before everyone else.

Our assigned role for a given evening meant we had to keep things moving in a certain flow. The dishwasher needed to wash things in the right order to give them a little time to drain, so the dishes weren't soaking wet when the dryer picked them up. But this also needed to be done in such a way that the dryer could access the driest dishes first.

And it was much easier for the person putting things away if the dishes were dried in a sequence that made this task more straightforward. I mean, why dry a few plates and then cutlery and then a pan, and then go back to plates? It just doesn't make sense.

Unfortunately, I couldn't always be the person putting away; that's not how a roster works. It was another important lesson in being part of a team and sharing responsibility for tasks, even if what you've been assigned isn't your preferred role. Plus, I'm pretty sure I got just a little bit more pleasure on the nights when I did the job I enjoyed the most. In fact, learning to recognize what you like most in life means you can incorporate more of it in your living—even if that means putting dishes away.

DISHWASHING TOWARD RESPONSIBILITY

As a teenager just starting out at university, I landed my dream part-time job: working in a bakery down the road from my house. I've always been a keen baker and particularly love getting my hands into the dough. And, even more, I enjoy eating the end result.

This work gave me a different perspective on the importance of doing the dishes. I was behind the counter of the bakery. Depending on my shift, this meant getting the loaves out onto the shelves in the morning, looking after customers, tidying up during the day, or closing up at night. I never got tired of the first waft of fresh bread wending its way up my nostrils as I walked into work.

I progressed from washing and drying the plates and cutlery of my home kitchen to giant baking pans, big sharp knives, and lots and lots of scrubbing. I'd always been relatively meticulous when it came to dishwashing and almost loved the small accomplishment of scraping away the last vestiges of cooked-on crust. But this took on a new meaning in the bakery.

" "

IT HELPS
TO SETTLE
MY MIND

For one thing, I was doing the dishes in what I would describe as a trough rather than a sink, as it needed to be large enough to hold the baking pans. Then there was the whole issue of food hygiene. The pans needed to be really, really clean, with the threat of the food inspector hanging over us.

As I became one of the more senior members of staff, it was important to ensure we cleaned thoroughly. This was sometimes no mean feat in the middle of sweltering Perth summers. Hanging over a hot sink in a rather warm bakery for extended periods of time was not such an attractive option when you'd rather be sitting by the pool or on the beach.

I took this responsibility seriously and there was a strange kind of pleasure in being in a world so far removed from my lecture theaters and library study. There's an element of joy in completing small, if sweaty, tasks that can be started and finished in a finite amount of time when compared with open-ended hours of reading. I also liked the feeling of completeness at the end of the day when stacking away the pans into their rolling shelf units, ready to be covered again in the wee small hours by rising dough.

17

It's easy to let these moments pass by when we are rushing, rushing through life, but there is a beauty and joy in finishing a small task—if we allow ourselves the time to recognize it. It's also an important part of growing up, this owning, undertaking, and completion of tasks. It gave me the confidence to try more challenging tasks in the kitchen and beyond. It ultimately also helped fund the next stage of my life and a move toward independent adulthood.

DISHWASHING TOWARD INDEPENDENCE

My first lessons in doing the dishes proved to be very helpful as I grew older, including the sibling negotiation of swapping and rearranging roster roles as the reality of late-teenage social life took hold. These skills were invaluable for my first real foray into the world when, as a hope-filled 21-year-old, I packed my suitcase and decamped to London.

Sharing a house and kitchen with people who were practically strangers is a great stress test of any relationship. It also opened my eyes to other people's kitchen habits, fortunately none too disgusting, but, in the absence of a mom-condoned roster, there is an element of diplomacy and flexibility involved.

Fortunately, I can live with a little mess, as long as it's not growing mold and doesn't hang around for too long. (This was more of an issue in a future house I shared with others, but I won't go into that!) My first housemates were a pretty flexible bunch, even happy to do one another's dishes when they piled up. I've heard many horror stories of arguments and passive–aggressive notes involved in disputes about dirty dishes, but, apart from the odd flare-up, this wasn't too much of an issue in our house.

A few months later I moved into a studio apartment. I had my very own kitchenette, stove, and sink, and only my own dishes to do. I could even—gasp—not do them for a couple of days, and that would be okay. I'd leave my plates neatly stacked in the plastic dish tub, not something I'd seen in sinks in Australia, and wash them when I was ready. Since it was only me, this was never too many plates and it never got even close to full, not something that could have been said for the previous shared kitchen.

I especially loved my quiet time on a Saturday morning, often recovering a little from Friday night drinks with colleagues. I'd clean my tiny kitchen, make sure everything was stacked neatly away, and head to my local supermarket for my groceries. After growing up in such a large family, it was the first time I'd had a space that was completely my own, with sole responsibility for looking after it. And, even if there were occasional pangs of loneliness, it was glorious.

When I left that apartment six months later, it was cleaner and more orderly than when I arrived. I didn't need a roster or the pressure of housemates to keep me tidy, and sometimes I did leave the dishes for a day or two, but I found that I was actually okay with that. I knew I would never be as clean as my mom (how on earth did she manage that with five children?), but I found a way of living and looking after my studio apartment that worked for me. And I felt proud of this small achievement, which signaled a movement into the next stage of maturity and understanding myself.

"

THERE IS A BEAUTY AND JOY IN FINISHING A SMALL TASK—IF WE ALLOW OURSELVES THE TIME TO RECOGNIZE IT

"CLEAN ENOUGH
IS GOOD ENOUGH"

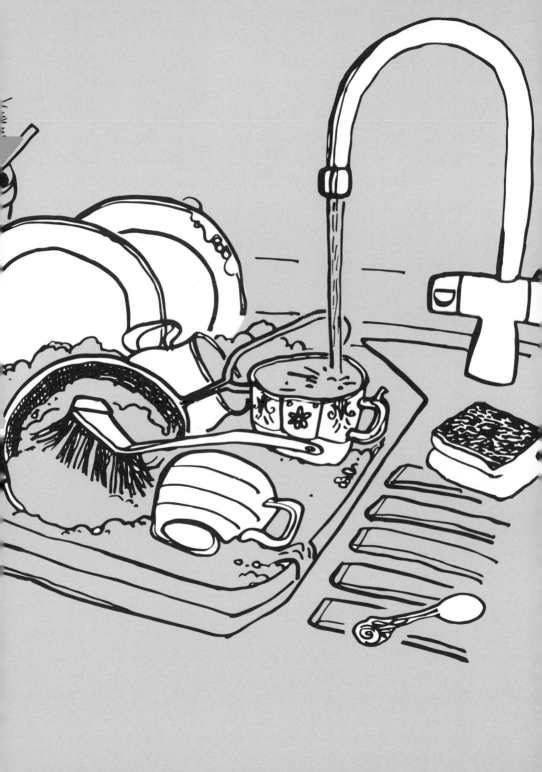

DISHWASHING TOWARD UNDERSTANDING

I mentioned the necessary orderliness when doing the dishes by category to keep the kitchen flow moving in the right order. In this, I'll admit to having perhaps a bit of a perfectionist streak about how the dishes "should" be done.

This includes the importance of diligently removing traces of food and fat, as well as considering the order in which dishes should be washed and stacked. It ensures that, for example, glasses get washed before other things so they don't get all the dirt from cooking pans and can be rinsed under the still-running faucet to remove dishwashing liquid. I've always done the cutlery next, followed by the plates, bowls, and so on, with larger items that need scrubbing at the end. You can see that I've thought about this.

However, while it was obviously important when dishwashing at the bakery for pans and utensils to be spotlessly clean, the question I had to, or was forced to, ask myself was: does this really matter quite so much at home?

Let me at this point introduce you to my husband, Johnny. Johnny does the dishes with gusto and, from the time I met him, has attested to his enjoyment of dishwashing (an important quality in a future partner). He genuinely likes the process of washing, partly I suspect because there are bubbles and splashing involved. For a long time he was quite resistant to our getting a dishwasher, even when we were planning our new kitchen, as he didn't see doing the dishes by hand as a hassle, and he kind of liked it, too.

However, he is also a little less concerned than I am about a tiny bit of dried food left on a bowl or a small smear of something on cutlery. Don't get me wrong, the dishes he did were clean, but maybe not quite 100 percent clean. At first it would bother me a little, and occasionally I'd make a little huffy breath to myself, or pointedly put something back in the sink to be done again.

Now, I'm not saying I'm the perfect dishwasher by any means, and my husband was definitely more likely to do the dishes than I was, particularly early on in our relationship. But I'd just notice if things needed a bit of extra cleaning while—I'll admit—sometimes being a little blind to my own "missed spots" and small cutlery smears.

But I have, over the years, learned a lot from my husband's approach. He gets genuine pleasure from doing the dishes, something which for me, if I'm honest, had until then felt like a bit of a chore. I've also come to the realization that clean enough is good enough. There's no medal or badge of honor for having the cleanest dishes in the world. And honestly, in the scheme of life, does a little streak left on a side plate really matter? I think we both know the answer to that one.

I didn't expect to learn tolerance through dishwashing, or to understand a little more about someone's personality from the way they do the dishes. I'm also grateful to have discovered someone with whom I can again share the dishwashing duties, who doesn't mind if I miss a bit when washing a fork. And even if my husband is a little prone to smashing things in his enthusiastic washing (which is why we have very few expensive wine glasses) that's okay, too.

DISHWASHING TOWARD BUSINESS

I think perhaps I've always known that my work would somehow end up in the kitchen. So many early signs pointed to it, including the way food and cooking filled my spare time. I knew that I didn't want to be a chef, the path chosen by one of my brothers, but that I really cared about how food and eating made people feel.

I love seeing people taste and explore flavors, and discover exciting combinations and delicious food that gives them pleasure. I now spend a lot of time in the kitchen developing recipes, preparing for my cooking workshops, and, on occasion, making products to sell.

In all of this, doing the dishes has taken on a new meaning for me. Partly it has become a meter to my day when I'm in the kitchen creating. I clean up as I go along rather than leaving everything to the end in a big pile. This keeps the kitchen in order and gives me a chance to pause and take stock, instead of rushing headlong into the next task.

If I've been standing up all day making chocolates, the final wash-down signals the close of my making. I now love the feeling of cleaning my tools, drying and putting them away, and looking over my spotless kitchen (perhaps this is also partly down to the influence of my husband's approach). It helps to settle my mind, which has been wrangling with chocolate temperatures and flavoring options all afternoon. It allows me a second to appreciate what I've created during that time.

Dishwashing is also the quiet time at the end of my classes. After the excitement of being around people and seeing what they have created, of the chatting and discussing, sipping and tasting, it is the chance to take a breath.

We now have a dishwasher (yes, my husband decided in the end that actually this was a good idea), so there are many things that I can put straight into it. However, there are certain items, the most precious, that still need to be washed by hand: my knives, my rough mortar and pestle, my baking pans, and my chocolate molds. I even have special cloths that I use purely for my work-related dishwashing, separating it from the normal household dishwashing.

Doing the dishes gives me order, it gives me peace, and it gives me faint memories of a noisy, food-filled household back in Australia that shaped the adult I've become. I am still working on just doing the dishes, while I am doing the dishes, but I'm learning to recognize and value the small moments that fill my day.

There is such a temptation to rush through small daily tasks like doing the dishes, particularly when they're repetitive and seemingly endless. We're always moving to the next activity, the next mouthful, the next meal, and perhaps feeling the small childhood groan I had at the thought of washing or drying the dishes.

However, in these moments there are opportunities to pause and reflect on the pleasure of a job completed. Yes, there will always be more dishes to do and more meals to cook, but at the point of doing the dishes there are just the dishes in front of you and a second to take a breath or two. Over time, we can even let these moments help shape us and our connections with others, as well as the acceptance and understanding of ourselves.

GET THE PLATE HABIT

Ideas for doing the dishes with joy!

1 | ONLY DISHWASHING
Could you get deeper and deeper into just the detail of doing the dishes? Can you let the distractions inside and out be simply acknowledged and allowed to be rinsed away?

2 | SHARING THE ORDER
What simple system and order to doing the dishes could you create alone or with your household? How might the tasks be simplified and the quality of the dishwashing improved? How does a little (perhaps shared) order feel?

3 | SUPER-CLEAN
When faced with a particularly tricky item to wash, notice how your mind considers the task in hand. What happens when you immerse yourself in the doing of a task with no end in mind? How does super-cleaning feel?

4 | DISHWASHING LOVE
Could you think of dishwashing a small way to take care of yourself? This is time taken to make your home healthy and clean. Could this be seen as a small gesture of love for your household and you?

5 | JUDGMENT-FREE
If you share the house with others, can you observe how they choose to do the dishes without judgment? Can you just notice and smile at the quirkiness of your different approaches and let any frustrations go?

6 | CLEAN AS YOU GO
Could you clean and tidy a little more as you go along? How does it feel to keep a level of orderliness? How does this affect your work and mind in the kitchen? Could this be effective elsewhere?

FLUFF & DUST

CHAPTER 2

FLUFF & DUST

Cleaning with meaning

Antonia Thompson | Artist at Phoenix Brighton and
former Editor at Huffington Post, AOL, Sky, and ITV

The bathroom light hits me like the dazzle of unexpected sunshine on a cloudy day. Someone sneaky must have left it on before I set off to drive the kids to school. Definitely a message: I've been telling myself I'll clean the bathroom for a week and still haven't got around to it. It doesn't really look that dirty, I have actually been giving the sink and floor a wipe now and then, I just haven't properly cleaned it with rubber gloves and scrubbing.

I am distracted by the purple fluff at the edge of the stairs. Why is it always purple? Who in our house is purple? Our carpet is camel-colored. I don't actually like purple. I can go as far as to say I own nothing, particularly of the woolen variety, that is purple. I kneel down and start scraping the fluff off with my hands; I could be here a while.

GIVE YOURSELF A BREAK FROM THE RESISTANCE

I lived with many housemates in my twenties and was often applauded for rarely leaving mess in communal areas or smelly food in the fridge. But when a housemate would utter the immortal words, "let's all clean up this place together," I would freeze and right there a familiar recalcitrance would fall over me; my rebellious, "don't tell me what to do," inner voice would kick in.

The more you resist something, the worse the feeling gets, the more you think about it, and the bigger and more out of proportion it becomes. But why give

28

" "

I'VE BEEN
TELLING MYSELF
I'LL CLEAN
THE BATHROOM
FOR A WEEK

something that is as innocuous and inevitable as cleaning the time of day in your valuable headspace? Save it for something really important like the utility bills, or, better still, learn to see past it.

Over the years, gradually, I've learned that if I acknowledge my ability to procrastinate, I can laugh at and overcome my immature behavior. The resistance is still there but I don't really see the point of living in a dirty, cluttered house. When things smell nice and there's some space to think, I just feel better.

KEEPING YOUR EMOTIONS IN CHECK

Getting beyond procrastination can be a struggle. According to scientists at Carleton University in Ottawa, Canada, if your mood is low you may habitually try to make yourself feel better by not getting on with a job you perceive to be dull or difficult. Unfortunately, this is merely a quick fix and you may be adding guilt to your already negative emotions.

Taking my own advice, I did get back to the bathroom, and during a flurry of plughole scrubbing I admitted I felt a little anxious. Exploring the plughole further, I realized that the root of my anxiety was guilt—guilt at having left my daughter at school in tears. (My partner has been working away from home for a week and she is really beginning to miss him.)

I let myself acknowledge the feeling, and knowing my child is well looked after and that she will no doubt come bounding out of class with a beaming smile on her face later, I let the feeling go.

EMBRACING IMPERFECTION

There is always something to do around the house: a solitary coffee cup, toys to put away, infinite coats and sweaters to put away, laundry to hang up, shoes to assemble in neat rows (you'll be lucky), garbage to take out, tables to wipe, couch cushions to plump up, and don't get me started on dust. My routine has evolved into cleaning and tidying up as I go, and most of the time that works. It helps me to not get too overwhelmed when faced with a large job.

Occasionally, however, it can feel like I'm always tiding up. When this happens, I know it's time to go on strike and let things get messy.

Making breakfast this morning, I ended up trying to peel a boiling-hot egg, with a burst yolk (don't ask), which became an extremely messy procedure. On a bad day I'd berate myself, but I chose to giggle and embrace my shambolic efforts. I even took a photo—various shards of shell, dirty spoon and egg remnants on one side, and smashed egg on toast on the other.

Life is messy, and living it to the full can be very untidy. Emotions, possessions, bodily functions, it's all one big colorful mess. There is so much going on in contemporary life and we have so many options and ideas available to us that it's easy to be overwhelmed.

"DURING A FLURRY OF PLUGHOLE SCRUBBING I ADMITTED I FELT A LITTLE ANXIOUS"

So accept the untidy and welcome what you can do about it. The act of acceptance can help you create the space to carry on enjoying your life. Leave a full sink and some eggshell on the kitchen counter if you want, trusting that later you will clean it up with gusto.

SIMPLE THINGS CAN MAKE ALL THE DIFFERENCE

I love my vacuum cleaner. When I got it I became instantly evangelical about how it had "literally changed my life." I was an advertising agency's wet dream, the millennial equivalent of the crazy Shake 'n' Vac woman from the 1980s. What's the big deal? The fact that it is cordless means the battery only lasts 20 minutes, so once the power has died, I have no choice but to stop. Guilt-free vacuuming: everyone should try it.

The joy of this fixed time limit is not new—Zen Buddhist monks have been doing it for hundreds of years. They practice something called Soji.

" "

HAVE YOU BEEN DOING YOGA FOR YEARS BUT STILL HAVE <u>PROBLEMS</u> <u>RELAXING</u> UNLESS YOU'RE IN A CLASS?

At cleaning-up time, all the monks are assigned separate tasks. A timer is set for 20 minutes and everyone has to clean to the best of their ability for the duration. The only rule is that they must be in the moment, and mindful of doing the task well and at their own speed. It doesn't matter if they finish the job or not.

When the bell rings and time's up, they have to put down their dusters and that's it. The idea is that the cleaning is done mindfully and whatever realizations they may have had during their meditation they should have activated into their whole selves through cleaning.

Now, I'm not saying vacuuming has made me hugely enlightened, but it has liberated me from the stress of the never-ending nature of cleaning. (For more about Zen Buddhism, see page 126.)

TRUSTING YOUR OWN EXPERIENCE
I have never really understood why issues I had as a child that I thought I'd dealt with resurface at peculiar times for no apparent reason. Until now.

The three-stage evolution of the human brain means that we actually have three brain sections, each fulfilling a different function: reacting, feeling, and thinking. Unfortunately, the reacting and feeling parts of your brain aren't that great at understanding the passage of time. This revelation, that the brain has trouble differentiating between things that happened years ago and things happening now, has been really useful to me.

When applied to a daily task like cleaning, my inner child will probably enjoy getting messy and won't see the issue with being untidy. My teenage self, like me, saw tidying as futile. My early-adulthood self still thought cleaning was very uncool, and my thirties cohabiting self enjoyed a wonderful foray into minimalism. Now my parental self sees a clean and tidy house as a basic human right for a child in the West.

This might explain why the grown-up me resists my partner's plea to hang my coat up. I may be experiencing a sense memory of having a fight with my mother about leaving my schoolbag in the middle of the kitchen.

Frankly, all this brain stuff is just funny. This is when laughing at and acknowledging your personal habits can really help with getting going with the cleaning.

UNEXPECTED BENEFITS OF CLEANING
However your own relationship to cleaning has evolved, it's worth exploring some nice surprises you might experience along the way.

Relaxation
Have you been doing yoga for years but still have problems relaxing unless you're in a class? Perhaps you aren't even aware of the tightening of your jaw when you vacuum or make the bed or get out the iron. Maybe you run, to get away from the problems of your day, and then later, for a reason unbeknown to you, you're unable to sleep.

I only realized I'd not been very clever about my yoga practice when I got injured and couldn't go to class anymore. I had been outsourcing my stress in a hot yoga class but not using what yoga taught me in everyday life. Waiting three times a week to fit in that 90-minute class to relax and let go, I hadn't noticed the tension building up in my body.

When I was injured and forced to become aware of my normal posture, I began learning to relax in everyday life without the help of yoga. I discovered that often my shoulders were tense when I was standing at the kitchen sink, and, even worse, I was holding my breath.

Learning to be mindful when fulfilling a seemingly mindless activity is a great way to bring softness and relaxation into your daily tasks. Taking deep breaths and stopping mid-task to acknowledge being in the moment can turn cleaning into a form of meditation.

Inviting happiness into your home
The Chinese believe that welcoming chi, or the "cosmic breath," into your home through Feng Shui can make you happier. By cleaning and decluttering regularly you can balance the flow of yin (feminine) and yang (masculine)

energy in your home. When there is less clutter in your home, you are making space to create, to think, to entertain, and to enjoy life. Whether you believe in the chi or not, it's a useful concept to be aware of.

Freeing up space to be creative

While getting messy or letting yourself be untidy can help with the creative process, starting with a tidy space can be very beneficial. A friend of mine who is a standup comic finds it impossible to write until he has completely tidied the kitchen and living areas. He needs to make space for the creativity to flow. Once the ritual of tidying is complete, he takes a deep breath, gets his notes out, and begins acting out his comedy ideas to an imaginary audience. He uses his clean space as his blank canvas.

> ## "WHEN THERE IS LESS CLUTTER IN YOUR HOME, YOU ARE MAKING SPACE TO CREATE, TO THINK, TO ENTERTAIN, AND TO ENJOY LIFE"

It's good exercise

When you do actually get into the cleaning, do you start to get a bit of an adrenaline rush? Do you feel a random muscle ache that is unfamiliar? That probably means you're also upping your fitness levels by cleaning well. It's a really simple consequence, but as a form of all-important aerobic exercise, it has a significant impact on our physical and mental well-being.

It can be good for your relationship

Sociologist Scott Coltrane has studied the division of labor in relationships and has observed that couples who equally share household chores feel happier. In particular, the effect of this fair division results in the female partner being more contented and less depressed. Coltrane also noted that women are increasingly citing as grounds for divorce male failure to contribute to a fair division of housework, so it makes sense to learn to share and enjoy cleaning up.

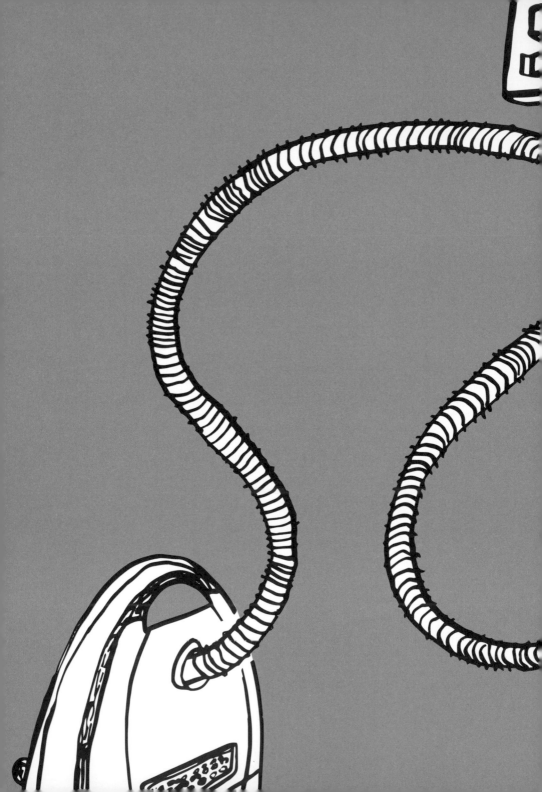

"LET'S ALL CLEAN
UP THIS PLACE
TOGETHER"

If your life is hectic and you and your partner rarely get a chance to spend time with each other, fulfilling household chores together can actually make your relationship better. The satisfaction of doing a job well while also looking after your joint living environment can provide mutual pride and satisfaction.

"FULFILLING HOUSEHOLD CHORES TOGETHER CAN ACTUALLY MAKE YOUR RELATIONSHIP BETTER"

My partner and I always do a quick tidy and clean-up before we go on vacation. That way it's always a nice surprise when we get home—it never fails to give me a boost after returning from a long, exhausting journey. So turn the music up and get the duster out. Or, if you can't make time together, surprise each other by doing the regular chore they might do daily.

It's appreciated by others, so you make a difference, one dirty plate a time. In 2017, the owners of one of the world's best restaurants, Noma, made their dishwasher Ali Sonko co-owner of the restaurant, recognizing his hard work and unfailingly positive attitude as vital to the restaurant's success. Clearly, in his 14 years of service, Ali's contribution has been important, however menial it may seem to other people. The recognition of his work is a tribute to that.

We can all learn from this that by focusing on the happiness of others, we can often make ourselves feel happy.

GET THE FLUFF & DUST HABIT

Ideas for cleaning with meaning

1 | CLEAN INTENT

Intention is everything, perfection is not. It's not about ironing underpants, but some people do that, and good for them. Notice how you are feeling when you clean. Is there tension in your body? Feel it and let it go.

2 | RESISTANCE

Set realistic goals. Try not to overwhelm yourself by saving up all your cleaning for one morning a week. Tidy as you go along. If you encounter resistance, remind yourself to clean now and avoid grappling with guilt.

3 | CLUTTER MANAGEMENT

If you want to declutter, try doing it one box at a time. When you buy something new, look and see what you can throw away, otherwise you soon won't be able to find anything when you need to.

4 | INNER VOICES

Use the voice of your parents if it is helpful. If it isn't, concentrate on one of your senses to allow that inner critic to take a back seat. Act on your instincts and niggles. If you dislike the smell of garbage cans, clean them.

5 | CLEANING TOGETHER

If you find yourself frustrated by others' cleaning habits, try setting an example and clean for your own emotional health and happiness.

6 | CLEAN PERSPECTIVE

Remind yourself of how far you've come in your cleaning journey. Remember that cleaning is a tiny part of a much bigger picture. Don't let it get it out of proportion.

TIME FOR A CHAT

CHAPTER 3

TIME FOR A CHAT

A guide to Western tea drinking

John-Paul Flintoff | Speak Listen

When I was a child, my father wrote a story about marital aids, and it was broadcast on national radio.

We all sat around listening. And this had a profound effect on me, if not perhaps in the way you might expect.

But before I tell you about that, I want to share something else—about how I make and drink tea. My own take on the "Western tea ceremony," if you like. As you read it, you may find yourself strongly agreeing with me. At other times you will disagree. And that's okay.

But before you go further, can I make a suggestion? Go and put the kettle on. Make yourself a drink so you can compare notes as we go along together.

Ready?

Great. Here goes:

When I boil the kettle, I tend to stand nearby, facing in a generally kettle-ish direction, as if that helps.

If the radio is on and something grabs my attention, I might turn the noisy kettle off briefly, till the radio loses me again. Then I might turn the radio off, and the kettle back on.

"　"

IT'S BY HEARING NEW THINGS, AND SAYING NEW THINGS, THAT WE CONTINUE TO GROW

And then I might be a bit more mindful about the whole tea business.

I wasn't allowed tea (or coffee) till I was about 11. In contrast, there's a photo of my wife, Harriet, clutching a cup of brown liquid aged about six.

When we met at university, Harriet did something that nobody else I knew at that time did: she went out for afternoon tea, not once but often. The first few times that I joined her, I felt like I had suddenly become a character in a novel by Evelyn Waugh or Henry James. (We were studying Eng. Lit.)

Today, I possess three teapots: one large, two small. They pour equally well. My favorite, a birthday present, has a lid on a hinge.

Alas, the hinge is worn, and the lid frequently falls in with the dirty dishes.

Hand-diving for it in the sink, I often find other people's dead tea bags. I remove them, squeeze them out, bury them in the food compost bucket, and wonder for the umpteenth time if I am the only householder capable of this sacred rite.

Looking in the cupboard, I notice, among the herbal teas, one called Womankind. Because of its name, I simply wouldn't dream of drinking it, ever.

I do occasionally drink other herbal teas. Sometimes regularly. But none of them draws me with the fierce addictive allure of what I'm going to call (bear with me) "normal" tea.

Yesterday, out of idleness and curiosity, I ranked my mugs in order of preference. I lined them up on the floor in the kitchen, and noticed that in a small number of instances I would rather *not* have a cup of tea than use them. But I still love the people who gave them to us.

I have no objections whatever to drinking from mugs that are chipped.

When I (very occasionally) drink out of a cup and saucer, I seem doomed always to be knocked by somebody walking past, causing tea to flood the saucer, then drip off the bottom of the cup onto my lap/top/laptop. I rarely spill from mugs, which suggests to me that saucers provide false reassurance.

I once stole a silver teaspoon from somewhere, but can't remember where.

I like it, enjoy using it, and feel no remorse. It's in the cutlery drawer, along with the stainless steel.

As a student, I shared a house with six others. The kitchen was adjacent to the bedroom of a medic, who once broke off studying for exams in order to denounce the rest of us for making too much noise. Not by talking, but stirring our tea: pling pling pling.

I don't have anything against making tea with tea bags, as such, as long as they are a) not removed too soon and b) not left sealed in a packet, while the water in the pot zooms to room temperature.

When I was young, I didn't care what brand of tea I drank. In fact, it's only been about three months since I started systematically to compare them. The results were surprising.

I strictly prefer whole cow's milk: unctuous and sour.

Lipton Yellow Label tea, it turns out, is not supposed to have milk added. I wish I had known that years ago: I could have been so much happier during vacations on the continent.

The ideal color of tea, for me, is probably Pantone 1385. I have a friend, a well-known journalist, who likes it at 1615. ("Too strong!" says Harriet, shocked, who prefers 138.)

Sometimes, when everything gets to be too much, I make myself a cup of tea and sit on the floor in the kitchen with crossed legs, cradling my mug, till I've rested my brain.

When drinking from a mug, I often absentmindedly find myself lowering the

"GO AND PUT THE KETTLE ON"

heel of my hand onto the top of the handle, then dropping my palm over the opening to the cup, keeping the heat in.

Note: I don't know why I do this.

If you write about your tea habits, and your tea history, and present it as a "Western tea ceremony," you might think you sound like the French essayist Montaigne, but the chances are high that you will come across like a silly snob out of a play by Alan Bennett.

This is partly because we take our own habits and ideas about something as everyday as tea for granted, and can't even begin to imagine that others would do things differently. You, reading my version, might be jumping up and down with objections, or improvements—but I have no idea what your version might be, and I suspect that your own grasp will remain hazy, at best, until you actually sit down to make notes.

And every note seems to bring up new questions.

For instance, I used the term "normal tea" earlier. But *my* normal may not be the same as yours, and if you came to my home and I offered you "normal tea" you might be horrified by the result.

I could say "English breakfast tea" but people drink it at other times of day, too, and in other countries outside England—and it's not grown in England either.

To avoid confusion with herbals, I could say black tea, but I have mine with milk.

I could specify Assam, Darjeeling, or Ceylon, but that's not right either.

This combination of complacency and lack of specifics applies to more than just tea, obviously.

With our everyday routines, we can become zombies, and blunder around for long periods of time until confronted with evidence that there are other ways to look at things.

Hoping for examples, I recently asked my friends about their own tea preferences. At first they were cagey, unforthcoming. One asked: "Is this a joke? A spoof?" I insisted my interest was sincere. And then it started to spill out—the many and various tea preferences of just one man's group of friends.

I laughed out loud when one told me this: "The bigger, the better in terms of mugs for me. Don't get me started on a teacup...detest them. Needs to be solid and have a proper handle."

I laughed, not because anything she said is particularly humorous, or controversial, but because what I enjoyed was the frankness with which she stated it. I pictured her, marching into a stranger's house and, when asked how she'd like her tea, saying exactly the same words: "The bigger, the better in terms of mugs for me. Don't get me started on a teacup...detest them. Needs to be solid and have a proper handle."

"WITH OUR EVERYDAY ROUTINES, WE CAN BECOME ZOMBIES, AND BLUNDER AROUND FOR LONG PERIODS OF TIME"

It might take them aback. Or it might just make them laugh, as it did me. It would certainly be helpful for anybody to know what she actually likes and wants.

There's a fine line between the satisfaction of having our expectations met and having them dashed.

Too often, when we go out to enjoy something we have perfected domestically, expectations are dashed.

Another friend told me she doesn't like being served large teapots with less than full measures of water, and she named the café where this happens a lot. Or drinking tea from bowls, as she's required to do in numerous cafés and coffee shops.

Worst of all, she despairs at the poor quality of the stainless steel in which tea is served at British National Trust properties. ("That actually makes me wild.")

In life generally, I suspect that the tendency to want and expect what we already like will only increase as technology gets better at presenting us with what it "knows" we like. For instance, it may not be long before we find that the most appealing content on Facebook is the advertising, because it will be so much better targeted at us than even a close friend's posts.

And that's fine—great, even, from a certain point of view. But I'm keen to pop my head out of the bubble of group-think and confirmation-bias every so often, and remind myself that there are other ways to look at things.

Not necessarily to agree with the disagreeable, but at least to hear it.

Because if our ideas aren't tested, we might as well die inside. It's by hearing new things, and saying new things, that we continue to grow. And I'm in favor of anything that can help us to do that, by having unexpected conversations.

I first learned this as a journalist, a magazine writer, traveling to interview all kinds of people I might never otherwise have met, and might have tried to avoid.

One time that sticks in my mind is when I was sent to Burnley, Lancashire, just after voters there elected councillors from the far-right British National Party.

I didn't go to Burnley expecting to like those individuals. But meeting the actual human beings, and hearing their life stories, was quite a revelation. It made it impossible for me to objectify them as mere specimens of a type.

The man I spent most time with was Len Starr, a former soldier, who ran a corner store. Over tea, in his back room, he hinted at various disappointments in life. As he did so, he didn't openly share his feelings, but didn't entirely hide them either.

And his tough exterior led him to walk into a—well, it wasn't *meant* to be a trap.

" "

THE <u>IDEAL</u> <u>COLOR</u> <u>OF TEA,</u> FOR ME, IS PROBABLY <u>PANTONE</u> <u>1385</u>

I asked him if he knew any of the "Asians" he kept talking about. "Of course," he said.

But it seemed he'd had only fleeting conversations with any of them.

"Have you ever been to the 'Asian part of town'?"

He said, "Not much—but I'm not afraid to."

So I suggested we go for a walk there. And he agreed. It was Friday, late afternoon. People were preparing for the weekend and lining up at the doors of retail outlets that had been converted into mosques.

I asked if he'd ever been to a mosque. "No, but I'm not afraid to," he said.

When we got to the door of one little mosque, the people there looked at us with suspicion, even hostility. What were two white men doing here?

I told them I was a journalist with the *Financial Times*, and left Len Starr to describe himself.

He said he was a councillor.

And they invited him inside, with newfound warmth and courtesy. I followed.

I'd love to tell you it was a beautiful Hollywood moment, where Len Starr became friends with all the people he'd previously distrusted.

But it wasn't.

He looked around, said hello in a low voice, maybe asked a couple of questions, and quickly stepped back outside.

But I respected him for going in at all.

And I enjoy the memory of his expression—a combination of awkwardness and respect that was so much more appealing than the know-it-all, lecturing style of the former sergeant and active politician I'd spoken with earlier.

Another time, I went to Belfast, Northern Ireland, to meet a former terrorist. I felt a little nervous traveling to see him, and stepping inside his headquarters. But he offered no violence. Instead, he offered tea, and I accepted, and I went with him into the kitchen while he boiled the water. I don't remember which way I orientated my body, relative to him and to the kettle, but I do remember that he took the bag out too early. The strong man made weak tea.

But, of course, I didn't say that.

Perhaps I should have done. Would it really have been so bad? It might have made him laugh.

On other occasions, I was sent to interview famous actors and directors over tea at upmarket London hotels. Taking notes in shorthand, my hands were too busy for the tea, but looking back I can see how important it was that it was actually served, that it arrived at the table, and was subsequently taken away.

"TEA PROVIDES A TIME AND SPACE FOR CONVERSATION"

It was important because tea provides a time and space for conversation, as Harriet taught me when we met at university. And at best, though not necessarily in celebrity interviews, conversation can change everything for the participants.

For them, and for us.

Whatever your own take on the "Western tea ceremony," it's a chance to find out something new. It can't protect us from awkwardness, but as a token of goodwill, tea can disarm.

It's irreducibly domestic, and familiar, even if you don't drink it yourself.

By writing this, I fear I may seem to be claiming some kind of special expertise. I'm not. But I have thought about it a lot. And I trace some of my fascination to that story my father wrote for the radio. It had an impact on me long before I started drinking tea.

In the story, as I remember it after so many years, a man was horrified by the opening of a new store across the road from his home—a store with the name of Marital Aids.

Being so young at the time, I had no idea why this was meant to be awful, but the writing was good, and it was clear to me that marital aids were meant to be shocking.

So I laughed with the grown-ups at the misfortunes of the uptight narrator.

But then (and I don't remember how) he was challenged to pay a visit to the store himself and, perhaps a bit like Len Starr when I challenged him to visit the "Asian area," he went along with it.

And so the story reached its climax as he went inside the store and found that it contained nothing risqué, only the kinds of things to furnish a happy home.

And the items that I remember best, all these years later, were a teapot, with cups and saucers.

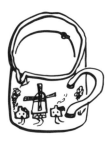

GET A TEA-DRINKING HABIT

Ideas for creating time for a chat

1 | KETTLE TIME

What happens while you wait for the kettle to boil? What do you notice about the sounds, sights, smells, and your emotions? Are there other distractions? Is this a moment when your mind can wander?

2 | TEA REFLECTIONS

Take a moment to notice your own tea-drinking rituals. What vessel and preparations do you prefer? What blend or brand attracts you and when? Can a twinkle of personal insight be unearthed?

3 | TEA FRIENDS

What do you notice about others' tea-drinking habits? What emotions do these observations trigger in you? Could you release any judgment and move toward just curious observation of little differences?

4 | AFTERNOON TEA

This can be a protected time dedicated to sharing tea and maybe a treat with friends, family, or even a stranger. Could cultivating a connection over afternoon tea become a feature in your calendar?

5 | FRANK TEA

Without heartless disregard for others' emotions, could you draw together your personal reflections, your observations of differences, and bring some frank and open sharing to afternoon tea?

6 | CONTROVERSIAL TEA

Maybe once a month, could you invite someone (or several someones) to share a cup of tea with you? Choose someone you wouldn't usually spend this time with. Notice what happens with the gentle offering of a hot beverage.

IMAGINATIVE WAYS TO LISTEN

CHAPTER 4

IMAGINATIVE WAYS TO LISTEN

Tuning in to the story

Ruth Williams | Department Store for the Mind

We all have moments of zoning out when we really should be listening. Maybe we get caught out with an unexpected question or perhaps we unknowingly miss a piece of important information. At home, with the familiar people in our life, it's so easy to switch off, assuming we've heard this before and we know where they're going with it. On busy days, when our heads are full of our own concerns, someone else's voice can all too easily just blur into white noise.

My other half, a head chef, often comes home from work with tales of less than helpful kitchen staff working against his desire to create the best food possible. The tales vary slightly but his levels of hurt and frustration are intense and heartfelt. He needs an ear and I physically make myself put down the things I am doing and turn my whole body toward him. I want to keep going with my own activities and offer only a cursory glance and the occasional nod while busying away. I resist this urge, but it takes a conscious move of my whole body to do it even though I've been talking about listening as part of my work for two decades!

To resist the urge to half-listen, I try to remember how it feels from the other side. What happens when we flip the roles over? How does it feel when you're sharing the story of, perhaps, your arch enemy from work, the funny anecdote you heard in a coffee shop, or the worry you have about your mother, and it seems to fall on deaf ears? Your stories are filled with your emotions, buried in

" "

BY TAKING TURNS LISTENING INSTEAD OF TAKING TURNS SPEAKING, YOU WILL BOTH BE HEARD

the detail of your story. The listener, whom you love and trust, should surely hear your heart—your joy, your pain, or your concern. How does it feel when they have missed the subtle clues completely? Worse, they didn't even hear the outline of the events!

WHAT GETS IN THE WAY OF YOUR EARS?

Many things can get in the way of listening. Often the greatest source for resisting listening is that your mind's inner chatter drowns out the other person's voice. Maybe we can zone back in occasionally, but what often happens in this situation is that we look for a connection, however tenuous, between our mind's inner chatter and their story, so we can jump in with a "funny you should say that, here's what happened to me today..." tactic and take over. This provides a chance to clear the inner chatter and talk about what's running through our own heads.

What happens next tends to be one of two things. Either the other person decides to forget about their own story and listen to yours instead or, more commonly, they treat you with the same level of courtesy and wait until they see their own potential for a tenuous link back to their story, then jump in. This odd game of taking turns speaking while no one listens is immensely common in adult conversation.

Sharing common experiences can be a lovely way to express empathy. However, here we are exploring what happens when our mind's inner chatter is interrupting our intention to listen.

What drives this funny game of taking turns talking is often the desperate need to be heard. Sadly, in striving hard to be heard first, no one is satisfied. Subsequently, the desire to be heard grows stronger and the willingness to listen fades further. So, the first step would be to quieten your own inner chatter and simply listen. "Easier said than done," you might say, but, as with anything, with a little practice we can all do it. Here's how.

Trying to stop or silence the inner chatter isn't realistic for most of us, but we can let the thoughts go as they come in. It's a practice people use in meditation that we can apply to conversations. When you notice a thought come creeping in, just acknowledge it, like someone knocking on your door. Mentally say to it, "I can hear you and I know that you're important and I will get back to you later." Then just let the thought drift away, and turn your focus back to your storyteller. The more you do it, the easier it becomes.

There is a wonderful, natural reward from this practice. When your storyteller feels heard and experiences what it is to be truly listened to, they are more likely to immerse themselves in your story once they have finished telling their own. By taking turns listening instead of taking turns speaking, you will both be heard.

THE MAGIC PAUSE

Busy lives where multitasking is commonplace leave little space for a pause. We carry this into our conversations. My friend Maria was fond of saying about conversations, "If the other person speaks as soon as you have finished your turn, then at some point they stopped listening and started thinking about what they were going to say next." This is a fun one to watch for in life. Over the next day, listen in to a few conversations and notice how often this is true.

So, what happens when we pause instead of speaking immediately?

There are two things that take place. First, you take a moment to consider what has been said. Second, the other person takes a moment to consider what they have said. A moment, taken by two people, to reflect and consider deepens the conversation and naturally strengthens the connection.

Just slowing down in your conversations is so powerful and yet wonderfully simple. It's the easiest way to find out what is going on for someone else. If you have a tricky discussion on the horizon, just try it. An added benefit is that the speaker has a natural desire to eventually fill the space and often will do so, without your needing to carefully craft a question.

"" "

WE
APPRECIATE,
DON'T JUDGE,
AND MOVE
FORWARD

YES AND...

This game is played by actors who improvise. It's good fun and leads to the most amazing creativity. The rules are very simple. You work with a partner by taking turns creating a story one line at a time. The rule is that your new line must begin with "Yes, and..." Here's what happens when you do it:

"The forest was dark and deserted..."
"Yes, and out of the trees emerged a creature with eyes like fire..."
"Yes, and the creature sighed and curled up to cry..."
"Yes, and he waited for his friend to arrive..."
"Yes, and..."

When we respond with "yes, and..." we are accepting what has just been said and are building on this. When two people do this together, they can reach creative insights at an astonishing rate.

The opposite to "yes, and..." would be "no, but..." or "yes, but... ." These usually happen when we disagree or are trying to win. If you look for something to agree with and build on this, rather than looking for something to disagree with, you can still have a different opinion while staying in the "yes, and..." mind-set.

The intention we have when we use "yes, and..." is that we appreciate, don't judge, and move forward. Imagine how it feels when someone listens to you with that intention. Even though we might not say "yes, and..." every time, we can have this in mind.

At home with our children, my partner and I try to create a "yes, and..." approach to conversation and interaction generally. Even though they are still small, we can see how this has boosted their confidence. We are still working on doing this more with one another, but I firmly believe that the closer we get to it, the happier and lighter our home becomes.

LISTENING WITH OUR EYES?

George, is a close friend who regularly joins us for dinner. He is an extraordinary individual. As an expert in a very complex and specific technical area, he knows things about his subject that reach such depths that he is the only person in the world who possesses this particular knowledge. The conversations over dinner can sometimes be quite unusual.

The art of hosting a dinner party is to help the conversation flow. Sometimes, George wants to talk at great length about technical details. If I'm not careful I can find myself zoning out. I need a way back in so I can connect and listen. I use my eyes.

A huge part of communication is about what we do with our body. Research shows that this is a bigger part than what we say with our words. Everyone has their own patterns and habits with regard to how they use their body when they communicate. These patterns provide a rhythm, punctuation, and elaboration on the teller's story. Seeking them out is not only fun but also deepens the insight you can glean and the understanding you can share.

You can look for different things in physical communication, but one of the most revealing is the individual's typical pattern and a change in that pattern. For example, at one of our family dinners George was telling me all about his work with the materials used to coat submarines. He tends to keep his hands fairly still when he speaks. I heard all about the materials and experiments in detail and then George moved to a story about how he had spoken to the naval customer, a senior figure, about his work.

His hands suddenly became animated, and when he mentioned how this tricky customer had responded to his suggestions positively and with thanks, he momentarily tapped his chest. This tap suggested a personal pride in his achievement. George had shared with me a story of something that awakened deep pride in him, and even though his technical knowledge was immense, it was actually this moment with the customer that he felt most proud of. Throughout the evening we discussed this more, and George eventually shared how tough communicating with these senior figures could be for him.

It was only by watching for a change in George's pattern and waiting, like a detective on a long, drawn-out stakeout, that I discovered the treasure, the personal insight, and a way to understand and connect more with George.

" "

YOUR STORIES ARE FILLED WITH YOUR EMOTIONS, BURIED IN THE DETAIL OF YOUR STORY

The chest-tapping moment had been brief, and if I'd been listening only with my ears I would have missed it.

When we share our living space with people, we subconsciously learn their patterns of body communication. Sometimes we will feel that our instincts have detected a change, but it will be more a case of having seen something different. By observing this more consciously, we can understand and connect more with those we love. It's also a great way to stay interested when the topic might be tempting us to drift off toward other thoughts.

SEEING THROUGH THEIR EYES

Mahatma Gandhi was famous for entering meeting spaces an hour or more before the meeting started. He would sit in the chair of each world leader in turn and imagine himself to be that person. He would play out the meeting in his mind and consider what thoughts would be in the head of the person he was imagining he was. In this way, when the meeting took place he had primed himself to be ready to understand the drives, emotions, and needs of each person. It didn't matter if his imagined thoughts were correct or not, he had simply shown an intention of seeing the situation from their perspective, and this carried through into how he interacted with them.

When we get a sense that someone else is really trying to see the world from our perspective, we feel willing to tell them more. They will listen more completely and ask questions that dive deep into the heart of our thinking.

Just like Gandhi, we can take a little time to consider what the world might look like from another person's eyes before we embark on discussion. The more we feel angry, frustrated, or hurt by that person, the more important it is to spend time doing this. If two people, in a potentially tense conversation, make an agreement to both pause and take a moment to explain how they see the situation from the other person's perspective, with (at least momentarily) no mention of their own view, the impact can be astounding. Next time you find yourself in this position, suggest taking a moment to trade roles and try it out.

THE BEST OF INTENTIONS

Harry, a friend of mine and father of three, recently shared how frustrated he felt that his child, Stella, was not doing as she was told and putting away her toys at the end of each day. During a chat over coffee after dropping the kids at school, he said, "I explain the reasons in three different ways but still she won't do as she's told." Even if you don't experience this frustration with children in your life, the chances are that you have a story of a situation with a friend or colleague at work where you've provided your argument and reasoning several times and they still just do something totally different.

Consider, for a moment, what is in Harry's mind as he approaches his daughter Stella to provide her with direction. He is probably thinking something like, "I have a sensible reason for wanting her to put her toys away. If I had been presented with that reason, I would have done it. I am sure if I explain it fully she will understand." This seems reasonable but Harry has missed something that could be a huge help to him. What about Stella's ideas and reasons?

Here's another way to look at it. Think about using forces (pushing and pulling) to move objects as an analogy for influencing someone's thinking. Harry wants to move Stella from where she is now to where he wants her to be with regard to putting her toys away. He does it by starting at where he is. He is then surprised to find that Stella doesn't move. He is simply in the wrong location pushing an imaginary object into empty space. If he wants the object (Stella) to move, he needs to be next to her or next to her thinking.

The solution is simple. Start with an open question and discover what's going on for the other person. Keep showing you're listening and continue asking questions until you discover where they are and what they're thinking. You then have all you need in order to shape your request in a way they will hear.

Harry tried this out with Stella. He discovered that he was asking her to put her toys away when she was in the middle of her game. After a little discussion, she agreed to put them away when she had finished playing. The game lasted for two whole days but Harry kept his patience. Sure enough, Stella was true to her word, and eventually put her toys away when she was done.

Put very plainly, begin by asking and discovering before requesting or demanding. It works almost every time and will save you huge amounts of frustration.

DO IT FOR YOURSELF

We have explored conversations with other people in our home and family lives and how we can use simple techniques to connect more closely and gain insight. It is possible to apply this thinking to the conversations you have with yourself—your inner chatter.

- If you have many things stopping you from listening to yourself, try getting them all out first, maybe through writing a list. Then consider each one separately in turn. Aim to do this in a quiet space free of interruptions.

- You can create your own magic pause in just the same way. Let one thought in at a time and reflect on this for a while before you move on to the next. If another creeps in, trying to interrupt, just acknowledge it and let it drift away.

- Notice how much you use "yes, and…" and "no, but…" as part of your inner dialogue. When an idea emerges, do you tend more to act on this ("yes, and…") or are you more likely to hesitate, finding potential problems with the idea and reasons not to act ("no, but…")? Could you use the "yes, and…" approach a little more?

- How aware are you of how you move your body when you think about different things? Could you notice this more? What thoughts make you smile? What triggers you to cross your arms and frown? What is this telling you about how you truly feel?

Taking the time to listen to ourselves and show self-compassion will also help calm down our own inner chatter and make us a better listener. As a dear friend of mine says, "Tend yourself; tend your world."

GET THE LISTENING HABIT

Ideas for tuning into the story

1 | BODY LISTENING
Could you physically put down what you are doing and turn your whole body to face the speaker? See if this helps remove tempting distractions and send a "listening" message.

2 | INNER CHATTER
While you are listening, if interrupting thoughts appear in your mind, can you try to acknowledge them and let them drift away? As you do so, can you simultaneously focus even more deeply on the speaker?

3 | UNDERSTANDING FIRST
If you are attempting to influence someone else, could you start by finding out their position, opinions, and feelings? Could you shape your request based on your discoveries?

4 | MAGIC PAUSE
Can you create a pause between taking turns talking in conversation? What happens when you do? How does the connection, pace, or content change? How do you feel about the time?

5 | YES, AND...
Can you turn your mind on to notice when you say, or are about to say, "No, but..."? Could you flip this to "Yes, and..."? What happens if you do? How do you react to the same? How might you encourage a change?

6 | GANDHI'S EYES
If a tricky conversation is on the horizon, spend some time preparing by imagining yourself in the shoes of the other person. How do they feel? What do they think? What is their ideal outcome?

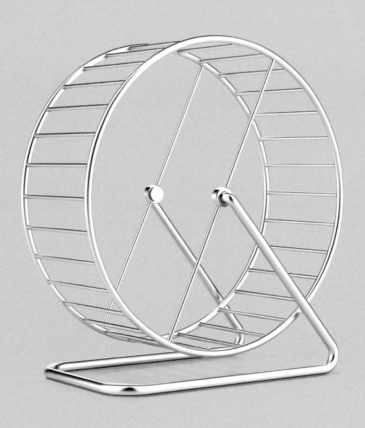

SUNDAY NIGHT BLUES

CHAPTER 5

SUNDAY NIGHT BLUES

Get to work

Kate Peers | Mad About the Boys

The weekend has been action-packed. Drinks with friends, running club on Saturday morning then lunch by the river with family. Sunshine, swimming, a movie, and the simple joy of reading the Sunday newspapers. Suddenly that blissful state is altered, those thoughts change, and a niggling feeling creeps in. We keep looking at the clock: time is running out. The Sunday night blues are creeping in and our mind turns toward the impending doom of the week ahead.

DO YOU SUFFER FROM THE SUNDAY BLUES?

Maybe you are lucky enough to have a job that you love and you look forward to going back to work. Perhaps your children have exhausted you to the point that you are secretly looking forward to sitting on the morning commute. For many, however, Sunday night is a reminder that a five-day stretch of work is about to begin. The daily commute, the long meetings that you dread each week, traffic jams, and exhaustion—work can be challenging in many ways.

How can we banish the Sunday blues? Sunday night may be the time when you end up daydreaming about quitting your job, making a total career change, or selling up and traveling around the world. The reality is that for most of us we cannot sell up and travel for the rest of our lives. So how can we make our Sunday nights better? Is it possible to avoid the sinking feeling and that overwhelming shadow of the week that looms ahead? What can we do to change how we feel?

"   "

WE NEED TO
BE AS INTERESTED
IN <u>BUILDING THE</u>
<u>BEST THINGS</u> IN
LIFE AS WE ARE
IN <u>REPAIRING</u>
<u>THE WORST</u>

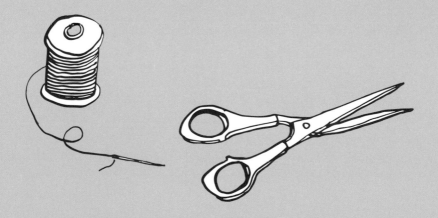

TAKING A LOOK INSIDE YOURSELF

The first obvious thing to do would be to take a look within ourselves, to examine perhaps what it is that causes us to feel this sense of doom about going back to work on a Monday morning. Traditionally, psychologists have spent time looking at why people are unhappy, where they may be going wrong in life, and what they could get better at. In 1998, however, there was a paradigm shift when psychologist Martin Seligman discussed, in his inaugural speech as president of the American Psychological Association (APA), the need to move away from looking at why people are miserable to learning more about what makes them happy. We need to be as interested in building the best things in life as we are in repairing the worst.

Think of a football team, in which each player has been assigned to a role that plays to their strengths. The quarterback may be incredible at scoring touchdowns, but that same player may be useless if positioned on the defensive end. Each player knows what their strengths are and they work hard to make themselves the best.

MAKING LIVES MORE FULFILLING

Psychologists have started to be as concerned with making people's everyday lives fulfilling, and with nurturing high talent, as they are with healing those who are unhappy. They believe that becoming happy and flourishing as a human being is determined by your circumstances only to a small degree, and that happiness is dependent to a much larger extent on your own intentional activities. This is not simply a pursuit for happiness; it is instead trying to focus on meaning in life, which in turn should make us more content.

WHY DO WE HAVE THE SUNDAY BLUES?

You may be wondering how looking at your strengths will help you have a more enjoyable Sunday, release some of the blues, and make you happier. I was, too, and it took me a while to understand the benefit of taking a look at our strengths and gaining a deeper understanding of ourselves and how we have a choice about the state of mind with which we approach things. I work from home so I don't commute, and I do a job that I love. There should be no reason for me to suffer from the Sunday night blues, but it still happens. Normally, it kicks in at about 3 P.M. when I begin thinking about the rest of my Sunday. Like a ticking clock running out of minutes, I feel overwhelmed at the tasks ahead. I need to cook a meal for the children, lay out their school clothing, bathe them (including checking them for lice, giving them a shampoo, ear cleaning, and nail cutting), listen to them read, and then read to them in bed, all by 7:30 P.M.

"THIS IS NOT SIMPLY A PURSUIT FOR HAPPINESS"

While the above tasks are being actioned, I am running through my work to-do list for the week ahead, which can include articles to write, deadlines to meet, and client meetings. A busy mind can lead to anxiety. After the kids are in bed, I write down my work list for the week and then begin on the household list. I make a meal plan, compile a grocery list, order the food online, and sort out the laundry. Exhausted, I head to the living room to sit down and try to read some more of the newspapers that I began reading hours ago in bed when I woke up. This is just my version of the Sunday night blues; each person has their own unique experience.

POSITIVE PSYCHOLOGY

Inspired by Martin Seligman's inaugural speech for the APA and his subsequent TED talk about positive psychology, I spoke with occupational psychologist Alison France. She is the founding director of Evosis, a company that helps individuals and companies with organizational strength, inclusivity, and culture change. Alison has seen firsthand how positive psychology can help create change, both in individuals and within groups in business. She suggested that I take part in an online test with the VIA Institute on Character. Based in Cincinnati, this nonprofit organization is dedicated to bringing the science of character strengths to the world through its research and online surveys. I took the VIA Survey to identify my signature strengths and understand how I could use them to help me day to day.

"A GOOD DIVERSION FROM THOSE SUNDAY BLUES"

""

EVERYONE NEEDS A GOOD BREAK IN THEIR WEEK TO AVOID BURNOUT

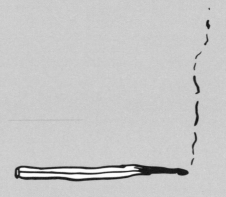

The test shows a total of 24 strengths. Everyone has all 24 but your top ones are what VIA refer to as your signature strengths. Finding out what mine are (humor, appreciation of beauty, and hope as it turns out) has allowed me to cultivate them in order to tackle the Sunday night blues.

The report suggested starting a humor diary to write down three things that have made me laugh during the day; with three young children at home, that is never a problem for me. I've always been drawn to the beautiful side of life and frequently get a feeling of awe and wonder from the buzz of a city or a walk in the woods. How can this help on a midwinter Sunday when daylight hours are minimal, it's cold outside, and the endorphins are a little lower than usual? An afternoon walk in nature each week, followed by a glass of red wine and healthy food could be a very good diversion from those Sunday blues, and there's the added benefit that appreciation of beauty is associated with mental health and life satisfaction. Hope, expecting the best in the future, and trying hard to achieve it are also important to me. Faced with Sunday chores and overwhelmed by the week ahead, my hopeful personality helps with resilience when facing challenges. One way that I've used this strength to tackle Sunday blues is to look back at other Sundays, examine what went wrong, and then find at least two positive insights gained from each challenge. The findings should give me hope that next Sunday perhaps things will be different.

USING YOUR STRENGTHS

Let's say that your strengths are kindness, creativity, and good judgment. You can probably come up with some good ideas about shifting away from the Sunday blues and replacing that time with something interesting, and this is all down to your creativity. The good judgment that you have will allow you to make decisions about how to help yourself, and your kindness will make sure that you think of others around you and how they could be feeling about your decisions.

There is a slight caveat, however, in that we often overuse our particular strengths and then they become a weakness. A classic example is when too much kindness leads to resentment, through trying to help others who haven't even asked for our help and then getting annoyed when they are not grateful enough. Maintaining a balance of our strengths is vital and is something we can look at on a daily basis once we understand more about the strengths we have.

PLAY TO YOUR STRENGTHS

I intend to use my strength of prudence to plan more effectively. I aim to get the school clothing ready and to write the to-do list for the following week on a Friday evening, when I am happy and feeling excited about the weekend. This gives me two less things to do on a Sunday night.

Having no commute to work can mean that it is hard to get going on a Monday morning. I am going to reframe this situation to remind myself how lucky I am to work from home. I plan to treat it more like an office environment, so I'll head out for a walk to a coffee shop in the fresh air first thing, treat myself to a delicious takeout cappuccino, and then head home to my desk, with a little treat to look forward to mid-morning.

Every person has their own reasons for having that feeling of dread that starts on a Sunday. It could be the job itself, not liking the person that you sit next to in the office, the train strike that's been announced for the following day, or simply feeling tired and not being able to think positively. Whatever the cause, you can help yourself feel better by fostering a feeling that things are more or less under control. Clean clothes, healthy food in the fridge, meals planned—all of these things help make our days run more smoothly, which will in turn increase our happiness. Avoiding scheduling any meetings for first thing Monday morning is also a good idea.

Avoid the temptation to sit down on Sunday and try to get ahead with work. No one can ever be that far ahead, and everyone needs a good break in their week to avoid burnout. There are enough other days to work hard. Embrace the Sunday-night feeling. Meditate, practice yoga, have a hot bath, and nurture yourself. Make Sunday a day to reflect and be kind to yourself.

GET THE STRENGTHS HABIT

Ideas for discovering Sunday night joy

1 | ONLINE FOCUS

Take part in online challenges such as 30 photos in 30 days on social media, which offers an opportunity to look at what makes you happy. You can create a lovely reference to lift any low moments.

2 | FRIDAY FINISH

Before finishing work on Friday, set aside time to plan ahead for the following week. Create a Monday to-do list, tag emails, line up necessary resources. Consider how good having a plan will feel.

3 | SATURDAY SWITCH

Switch your Saturday to a Sunday. We typically plan our fun activities for a Saturday and leave the more mundane tasks for a Sunday. Swap it around and notice the difference. Does it make the weekend feel longer?

4 | SUNDAY PLANS

Plan little treats throughout the day. Make your evening meal a really special occasion. Sunday dinner, served at the table and surrounded by family or friends, can brighten our moods significantly.

5 | GRATITUDE JOURNAL

Start a gratitude journal and, at the end of each day, write down and remind yourself of what you have been grateful for. On a Sunday night, give yourself a little lift by reading through the last week's entries.

6 | SUNDAY NIGHT RITUAL

Give yourself a new ritual for a Sunday night. It could be heading to a yoga class, or a family movie night. Keep this up every week and you will have given yourself something to look forward to.

VIRTUALLY HERE

CHAPTER 6

VIRTUALLY HERE

A guide to online presence

Clare Barry | Urban Curiosity

The cookie can is empty, which doesn't surprise me because it was empty the last two times I checked. Currently I live alone, so I shop for one and I do all the eating. I *know* there is not a cookie crumb in the place, but this logic does not prevent me from opening the cupboard and poking around just in case. I have this chapter to write and I've missed my deadline twice because I am an epic procrastinator, so this is not about having the munchies. I am searching for distraction; I crave something to fill a hole and provide a little pleasure hit to make me feel better.

COMPARISON IS THE THIEF OF JOY

Sugar won't help my word count, of course, and neither will Facebook. Still, I scroll through my feed the way I dunk a cookie into my tea (where, often, I mistime things and half my treat sinks to the bottom of the cup, making the last couple of sips a sugary, sludgelike disappointment). I soak up all the beach scenes, apartment layouts, and inspirational quotes available on Instagram then look back to my blank page with a queasy feeling in my gut.

My desire has not been sated and I feel worse now than I did before. My own feed does not have a coherent style or beautiful filters and I don't have loads of friends or likes or comments. My writing isn't as sharp and my compositions are dull. My sweet tooth is keeping me from a washboard stomach and I've just noticed how outdated my kitchen is.

" "

I KNOW THERE IS
NOT A COOKIE CRUMB
IN THE PLACE

On the whole I am happy with my life and the work I do (procrastination-related deadline pressure aside) and yet here in my home I'm struck with comparison paralysis. First I feel an ennui and then my thoughts spiral into a series of realizations that I am not doing enough; I don't have enough. *I* am not enough. Then I berate myself for my covetousness and vanity, my time-wasting, and shallow thinking. It seems like everyone has life sussed and I don't.

ON FAVORABLE IMPRESSIONS AND SEARCHING FOR THE GOOD LIGHT

The clue is in the verb "to seem." We share images and status updates to fit the story we want to project about ourselves. I take a selfie from my best angle and in a flattering light. I photograph my meal because I want people to know I cook Ottolenghi recipes. I elbow the junk on my coffee table out of shot so anyone viewing my Instagram or Facebook accounts will see only an expensive candle, fresh roses, and a highbrow book. I control my online image because I want to give the world a good impression and hide the real one with its frown marks and microwave meals, and messy living room.

This isn't much different from my shoving clutter into a drawer or pulling my greasy hair into a ponytail when my neighbors show up unexpectedly. We project the homelife we aspire to via our online personas. At present, I am working in pajamas on a Saturday night; my brother's reality is a weekend stuck at home looking after my nephew, who is unwell. And yet each of us may create or maintain a façade thanks to the devices at our disposal: he could imply a cozy family baking session with photos from a healthier weekend; I could suggest my finger is on the pulse by referencing the latest must-read novel.

Sometimes we experiment with new identities via our online selves. We can dip in and out of a stream of tweets about organic gardening or sign up for a hard-rock fan forum. In our online skin, we can be whomever we want, and when we are no longer interested we simply unsubscribe, unfollow, or stop engaging. We fade away without losing face in the way we might in the real world.

It is a human thing to show our best selves because we want others to think well of us, and when the truth isn't as attractive we contrive things. If we are striving

for the perception of perfection in our online presence, so are others.
It is curious, then, how we judge ourselves against such unfair benchmarks.

RESISTING TEMPTATION

More curious than comparing ourselves harshly is how we open up to these opportunities in the one place where we can take refuge from the noise of the outside world: our homes. We invite in the pundits and bigots, the showoffs, the gossips, the judgmental types, the chatterboxes and doom-mongers, the bosses, the know-it-alls, and the perfectionists. If any one of these individuals were seated at our kitchen table espousing unpalatable views or making us feel inadequate or bored, we'd ask them to go. But they are not and so we welcome them over the threshold of our online home and seldom ask them to leave.

The line between work and play has become blurred thanks to mobile technology and the internet, which allow us to be connected whenever we like, work from wherever we please, gain knowledge in a second, and never be out of touch. These advances were intended to enhance how we live and work, which they do in myriad ways. The problem comes when our behavior around, and our dependence on, our digital devices and accounts exacerbate our stress levels and negatively affect our well-being.

"WHEN THE TRUTH ISN'T AS ATTRACTIVE WE CONTRIVE THINGS"

Let's say we struggle to wind down after a long, busy day, and the frequent arrival of alerts and ringtone sounds, plus the sight of unanswered messages or unwritten articles, induces anxiety. Perhaps we crave connection or affection but prevent it by appearing to prioritize others or different sources of stimuli as we gaze at our smartphone in the company of an actual human being. We complete a life-admin task like online banking from bed at 10 P.M., and the temptation to click on something else is overwhelming. Soon it is 2 A.M. and we know more about a skateboarding YouTuber's antics in New York City than we needed.

Resisting the urge to check or click is a real challenge because, even though teams of smart people create devices, software, and platforms to help us, they also design these to entice us and keep us coming back. The pings and dings give us an endorphin hit each time they go off, and those messages telling us we have unread email make our hearts race in anticipation. Over time, as we sign up to more social media platforms and download more apps, we can find ourselves feeling overwhelmed and/or unsatisfied.

If we are to thrive in this hyper-connected world, we will benefit from getting to know ourselves better. This means understanding our motivations and intentions when it comes to our online selves; acknowledging our choices; and recognizing the benefits of having a place—our home—for literal and virtual peace and quiet.

"WE GAZE AT OUR SMARTPHONE IN THE COMPANY OF AN ACTUAL HUMAN BEING"

Here are a few experiments to help us be more present and aware of our actions in our online presence:

Reset the agenda and teach others what to expect
Let's take back control over our agenda and schedule. Turn off all unnecessary alerts and notifications. Place a ring fence around time spent checking online feeds and, in particular, responding to email. We can choose *when* to absorb what others think we need to know. The important part to note is this: what is important to the other person may not be so to us. All the more reason to put our own agenda, needs, and priorities first.

For example, I am most alert and creatively fired up in the morning, so I reserve this time for my core work and leave emails or meetings until after lunch. If a matter is urgent, then people can call me. I communicate this to them verbally or via an out-of-office message to help set their expectations of me.

Embrace boredom

The arrival of the internet and smart devices into the home means we no longer have to endure boredom. Patience while the kettle boils or the iron heats up, when the toddler refuses to eat their food, or commercials interrupt our prime-time viewing enjoyment is not required. We never have to be alone with our thoughts or feelings because that handy device is available to provide entertainment, information, and distraction. In avoiding boredom in these small slices of downtime, we miss opportunities for joy and contemplation, connection and insight.

When we engage in dull domestic tasks like folding laundry or loading the dishwasher or scrubbing pots in the sink while allowing our minds to roam, a reminiscence makes us happy, or we have a helpful realization. We open up to possibility in the moments in between: our spouse expresses tenderness or our child confides a fear or we share a vulnerability. Think about how many lightbulb moments occur in the shower. It is the last place, for many of us, where we can do nothing but enjoy the water running over us and daydream.

Often when we allow the pauses and quiet pockets of time into our domestic life, we are rewarded.

Know our why

We should question why we share what we share online and why we have the kind of relationship with our inbox that means we're handling work emails from the bedroom. If we are honest, we want some kind of external validation and to get another lovely rush when people like, retweet, or share our content. This is why it feels so disappointing—and personal—when our video of little Johnny receives no engagement.

What if we focus on our enjoyment of the act of writing, photographing, or deciding to share a link, and let go of any attachment to how any of them is received? It is about how the process feels rather than the result. Another approach is to think of our social media updates as an online record of our lives. How does it feel to take pleasure in compiling this record but accept we have no role in how it is received?

"IT SEEMS LIKE
EVERYONE HAS
LIFE SUSSED
AND I DON'T"

When it comes to the overflowing inbox, it can help to get clear about our motivation for sending an email. I ask myself whether I want to show myself in a positive light or cover my backside? Am I copying in half a dozen people just to look clever and connected to them? Would a phone call or a face-to-face conversation work better?

Do one thing at a time

Let's focus on monotasking in the home and online. We praise the technology that allows us to squeeze every moment out of the day as we walk, talk, and text simultaneously or sing nursery rhymes with our baby while purchasing an outfit online and pan-frying sea bass. We believe that technology helps us juggle everything, but all this multitasking can contribute to our feeling scattered and stressed out. It can also be inefficient. For example, our mobility when walking while talking or texting (but particularly the latter) is impaired; so our child senses our distraction and throws a tantrum, and we place the order but buy the wrong size, and dinner is cremated.

What happens when we deepen our focus and effectiveness by doing one thing at a time both in real life and via our online interactions? What about extending this to social media channels, i.e., use one only for a period of time?

"SHARING STUFF REACTIVELY AND WITHOUT THINKING JUST ADDS TO THE CLUTTER ALREADY FLOATING IN THE DIGITAL ETHER"

Be a mindful consumer and thoughtful curator

Snacking on digital junk can be the same as eating unhealthy food—shortly afterward we feel uncomfortable or bad, and not long afterward we are ravenous for something else. When we are deliberate in our consumption online, we take back control over the content that informs, inspires, or motivates us.

Discernment about what we consume also works when it comes to what we share with others online. Sharing stuff reactively and without thinking just adds to the clutter already floating in the digital ether. Becoming thoughtful curators of content, relating to subjects that matter to us, is another way of gaining an online presence that works for us and our followers and friends. Do they need to know what we intend to post? Will it delight or inform them or be thought-provoking?

Embrace the *joy* of missing out

What happens either side of the shutter closing and opening often tells a very different story from the one in the still photo. Once a status update, tweet, or image is shared online, it becomes static. These are minute impressions of our thoughts and experiences. Is my friend being dishonest by sharing an idealistic vignette and suggestion of a great night out when the reality was different? Yes and no. Does it really matter, though, if I know comparison is the thief of joy and I relinquish my fear of missing out?

When we accept that we can't be everywhere or know everything, we can embrace the *joy* of missing out, and feel liberated to relax at home, happily ignorant of whatever the 24-hour news cycle is saying for a few hours. We can let go of our ego and rest assured that the world will not stop turning if we stand still and don't comment on something. We care less about the event or revelation we missed out on and bring ourselves back to where we are now.

Seek meaningful connection online and off

We all know that person who makes us feel like there is no one else in the room. They offer us their undivided attention and it feels great. In reality, we shortchange each other much of the time. Time at home with our loved ones can feel better when we do one thing at a time, make eye contact, and welcome affection because we are present.

Online connection with people who matter to us can be meaningful, too; we have to be less passive in our engagement, though. For example, would we make more effort to telephone, Skype, or write to someone who lived far away, or even travel to see them, if we didn't feel connected to their reality because we liked their weekend photos on Facebook?

Can we truly know what is going on in someone's life by following their Instastories or watching their YouTube videos but never connecting with them in a more engaged and meaningful way? If the answer is yes, then the person is an acquaintance and not one of the small group of people who truly make a difference to our lives. When it comes to the latter group, let's nurture those relationships.

Being present means focusing on the here and now. Doing one thing at a time with intention—whether in real life or online—can be the path to feeling positive and calm, not stressed or inadequate. An online presence in our hyper-connected world is about being a conscious consumer and participant, not a passive bystander. When we are mindful of our most precious resources— time, energy, and attention—we become more intentional around how we spend them here and make different choices. It means that we understand whether a mooch on Pinterest makes us feel jealous or inspired, and that we have the choice to unfollow or hide a feed filled with opinions or facts that bring us down.

Remember who is in charge. We are.

GET THE ONLINE PRESENCE HABIT

Ideas for being much more than virtually here

1 | ALERTS & EXPECTATIONS

Switch off alerts on your phone so you check at specific times, one feed at a time. Check emails at intervals and let people know what you're doing.

2 | PERFECT BOREDOM

Between activities and events, what happens if you just pause and simply do nothing? If it's unusual for you to do this, begin with moments of quiet stillness and try to increase the time as you continue with the habit.

3 | ONLINE REASONS

Take a moment to consider why you post, blog, and upload the things you do. Perhaps instigate a discussion about it with friends. Is there a way that you can free yourself from seeking validation online?

4 | THOUGHTFUL CURATOR

Can you set yourself a few criteria for the things you post, upload, tweet, or comment about? Maybe consider how it inspires you or might shape the world you want to live in.

5 | JOYFUL MISSING OUT

With all the parties, events, and vacations that everyone else seems to be knee-deep in online, can you switch it off? Can you feel the liberation of becoming more satisfied with your own here and now?

6 | MEANINGFUL CONNECTION

Rather than maintaining hundreds of acquaintances, might you spend more time with a few valued friends? How might that connected time be different? How does the difference feel?

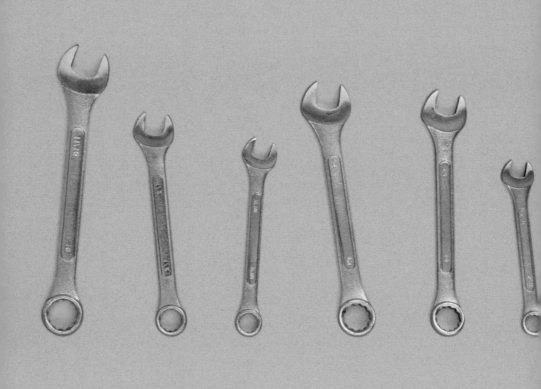

TAKING CARE OF YOUR STUFF

CHAPTER 7

TAKING CARE OF YOUR STUFF

The art of bicycle maintenance

Ruth Williams | Department Store for the Mind

My ex-boyfriend, Sam, tended to fixate on many things, but pedal bikes and how much stuff he owned were the two main ones. Now in my early forties and a mother of two, I can reflect on this time with new eyes. There was sense in much of what he obsessed about that I was less aware of at the time. First, let me tell the story of Sam's special ways.

TOOLS, CLEANING, AND FIXED WHEELS

At least once a month Sam would spend a day or more stripping down his bike completely. He would take great care in slowly and carefully cleaning every component. He had a specific set of tools that helped with the work. The tools were wrapped in a cloth pouch with a designated pocket for each tool. The choice of order was not random but considered, and was based upon the frequency with which the tool might be used and the sequence in which it would be required. The pouch was just the right size to fit everything in, and no pocket was left empty. It could be rolled up and tied into a neat bundle so all that was visible was the plain outer color (dusty yellow) of the cloth.

Each tool had a story and most had been given to Sam by someone with knowledge of and insight into the care of bicycles. The tool would have been passed on without any charge, and the giver had usually shared their knowledge with Sam as part of the exchange. Sam only kept exactly the number of

" "

EVERY MATERIAL OR ITEM WE USED HAD A FUNCTION, BUT THINGS WERE <u>CHOSEN WITH CARE</u>

tools he needed and would give away anything he deemed to be no longer useful. When he gave it away, it was with consideration and care as to who might need it and how useful it might be to them. He would, in turn, share his understanding about the use of the tool as part of the exchange. This completed a circle of giving and receiving that Sam believed allowed him to have just what he needed when he needed it.

When Sam engaged in this ritual maintenance of his bike, he did it alone. He would check the weather and choose a dry day. He cleared space in the backyard. He did not listen to music or chat as he worked. He thought about and prepared everything he needed in advance so that there would be no interruptions to the process. Oily metal components were cleaned in gasoline, and specifically selected rags had special roles. He took time and he thought about what he was doing. There was an expression of love and respect for his bike that Sam communicated through this activity. Afterward he was calm and peaceful. His bike always ran perfectly and provided him with exactly the transportation he needed.

"THE BIKE DELIVERED JUST WHAT WAS NEEDED AND NO MORE"

Sam rode a fixed-gear bicycle. This type of bike has no freewheel mechanism and is set up so that the rider must constantly pedal. You cannot freewheel on a fixed-gear bicycle, and among fixed-gear riders there is a connection and shared understanding of what it is to ride this kind of bike. The basic premise is that the type of riding means you are connected to the machine as one. As you pedal constantly, an uninterrupted rhythm is achieved that is affected only by the need to move faster or a change in incline. Gears and the opportunity for freewheeling would interrupt this style of riding. You are aware of the environment through which you ride without the interference of unnecessary mechanical additions. I tried it myself and, although it was a harder ride, once into the rhythm there was a sense of simply traveling that felt liberating. The bike delivered just what was needed and no more.

A PLACE FOR EVERYTHING AND EVERYTHING IN ITS PLACE

Later in our relationship, Sam and I converted a large van into a home and living space ready for him to stay in when he attended circus school in the southwest of the country later in the year. The design of the van was clean and simple.

Before we embarked on a day of work, Sam would gather and arrange the tools we needed for the job. They were stored in special trays and, without fail, at the end of the day's work, they were returned to their correct place. The jobs were not rushed and while we did this work we did nothing else other than eat and sleep. The quality of the workmanship was good and every detail was considered. Every material or item we used had a function, but things were chosen with care. We used materials from sustainable sources, in as unprocessed a form as was possible, and chose natural finishes for the walls and floor. It was a peaceful place to be. The pace was even and smooth.

RESISTING "STUFF"

Advertising, marketing, and often social media constantly send messages to tell us that who we are and what we have are not good enough. We are encouraged in many subtle ways to strive to change, often with the promise that through purchasing specific stuff we will discover happiness, wealth, beauty, an amazing partner, and happy children. The list goes on and on. But Sam religiously kept only what he needed. He had one large red-and-white duffel bag that he had carefully decorated and he never owned more than he could fit into this bag. If he found that he had too many clothes to pack into the space, he would give something away.

We lived together but he kept this bag packed. It left me feeling uneasy, as he spoke frequently of traveling to India again. I had a sense that with his bag packed he might leave at any time. If I raised this, he would say it was because he wanted to feel free to move, though this didn't mean that he would. For me this was less than reassuring. However, he literally had no material ties to weigh down his freedom. Reflecting on this now makes me wonder whether our accumulation of stuff could be a means to keep us within an environment that our instinct would have us leave if we were lighter?

" "

HE NEVER OWNED MORE THAN HE COULD FIT INTO THIS BAG

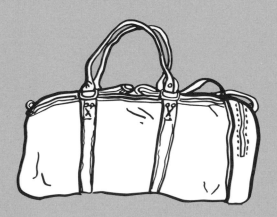

Maybe Sam's duffel bag is an example of the more extreme variety, but I do think carefully now about what I purchase. If I need to buy less, I need to earn less, and consequently need to work less, so I have more time. If that stuff is unnecessary, then it's a no-brainer to me to resist the subliminal messages and keep my wallet in my purse.

Here are a couple of things I do to make the resisting easier. As much as is humanly possible I avoid advertisements. I watch TV without commercials and never buy magazines that are filled with advertising. I get into the habit of checking carefully in my mind and with my partner about whether we really need something before we buy it. I am very careful with my use of social media, too. Even though friends, family, and acquaintances are unlikely to have the profit motivations of the people behind the marketing campaigns, they can be as influential in creating a thirst for shopping. Resisting is a mind-set that takes a little practice to adopt, but I find it liberating.

If we have less stuff, we need to maintain fewer things. Time is ours once more, and the opportunity to slow down and choose grows beautifully.

ONE THING AT A TIME
This is a recurring theme in this book. It is the heart of being present and the cornerstone of unearthing calm in everyday corners. Multitasking isn't even all that efficient. Research shows that when we do it, we do many things to an average standard with more mistakes.

This concept reminds me of a quotation from Robert M. Pirsig's *Zen and the Art of Motorcycle Maintenance*: "The place to improve the world is first in one's own heart and head and hands, and then work outward from there." Try immersing yourself in one simple maintenance task at a time instead. Notice each of the senses one at a time—the feel of the tools, the sounds around you, and the sounds of your task. For Sam it would have been the smells of the oil or gasoline or the scent of the flowers growing through the cracks in the slabs of our little backyard. Take a moment to notice the tones, the colors, and the multitudinous array of light you see. Feel a rhythm to your work and let that slow, even pace carry you through.

In daily life, we often have many things to maintain and a sense that we have more tasks to complete than time available. This is a wake-up call to check in on what you really need. Do all the things you maintain have a useful function in your life? Are they adding to your happiness or do they serve another purpose? What might you let go? Who might you pass this on to?

LEAN MANUFACTURING AT HOME?

In my late twenties, I worked for a while with Toyota on a consultancy basis and its very particular approach to how the organization was run fascinated me. People train and specialize in this approach and similar ways of working that have originated in the company's motherland in Japan. These approaches have some wonderful names I won't go into here, but most are grounded in the ideas of lean manufacturing. There were two aspects to what I learned of their way of working that resonated loudly, firmly, and deeply with me, and they continue to do so.

Doing the same stuff at the same time

First was the idea of achieving an efficient way of working by grouping similar tasks together. In doing this you can be free of what is termed "waste," meaning wasted resources, including time. One way of thinking about this is considering, for example, on an average morning at home, how many times you run up the stairs to get something you forgot to pick up on your last trip. If you wanted to reduce waste, you would slow down, take time to think, plan a little, and collect all the things you needed on one trip.

Applying this idea to the tasks you complete at home, grouping activities together can save you a significant amount of time. The manufacturing industry does this to create a smooth and efficient process.

Something more than an improved manufacturing process happened when the management gave the employees permission to slow down and take time to think and plan. The place was so calm. Meetings were connected and creative—it was refreshing. Focusing on the task at hand in the present just made it so much easier to simply be.

As I first stepped into motherhood I found myself juggling childcare, part-time work, and the maintenance of the family living space. It was then that I remembered lean manufacturing and began grouping activities together, simplifying the things I did and doing one thing at a time. I think it saved my sanity and helped massively in my becoming a calmer mom. The way you apply these techniques to your own home management is more about adopting the mind-set than, for example, arranging and folding socks in your drawer in a specific way. It's an ever-changing process, and creating it for yourself makes it easier to adapt. It makes me smile to think I am bringing car-manufacturing techniques into my home. I must admit it's not something I regularly discuss with other parents I meet in the playground, but maybe I should!

Quality in the hands of everyone

Second, a famous aspect of this approach is that every employee can stop the manufacturing process if they notice any indication of poor quality in the cars being produced. Even the most inexperienced member of the factory team can do this! Quality is king. When a problem is highlighted, everyone works together to find a solution. The blame game is not given a moment's space.

"QUALITY
IS
KING"

In the academic world and beyond, the debate about "quality" is vast. What I offer here, from my observations, is the effect it had on the atmosphere of Toyota's workplace. Giving this level of control to every single person put the focus on working well to deliver something every soul could feel proud of. There was no evidence I saw of hierarchy or competition between colleagues. People had a lightness and humanity with one another that I have never experienced on such a level before or since. Information was readily available and willingly shared. There was no envy or resentment that I witnessed or heard even the slightest whisper of. Again, it brought people into the present rather than their being focused on mistakes of the past. People were free to find solutions and were rewarded emotionally for doing so.

"EACH TOOL
HAD A STORY"

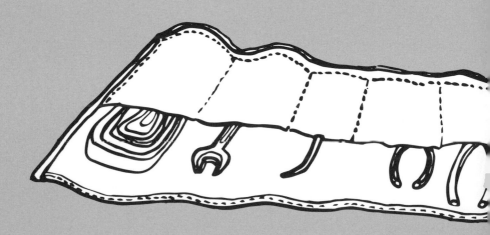

PROBLEM-SOLVING AND WORKING TOGETHER

How can we bring these attitudes and this approach into our homes and daily existence? First, if the tools and appliances we use within our homes are not working effectively, then we need to stop and take time to investigate how to solve the problem, rather than pushing through and ignoring the indications of a potential breakdown. We should try to work with what we have, rather than throwing out and replacing the item at once. If we have fewer things of better quality, then this is far easier to do.

Second, when things go wrong or break, we should focus our attention, and that of the people with whom we share our living space, on how to find a solution. Creating upset and resentment by searching out who is to blame breaks connections and increases the likelihood that someone might break the item again, this time on purpose (it would in my house anyway!). By working together to find a solution we all gain a greater understanding of how a thing works, we bond a little through the experience and, finally, we find a new respect for and understanding of the item we have maintained together.

GET THE MAINTENANCE HABIT

*Ideas for creating good relationships
with your stuff*

1 | TOOLS

Whatever the job, how can you choose your tools with care? Can you use fewer things of better quality? Who might help you choose and use your tools? How could you exchange your tools and knowledge?

2 | A PLACE

Where do you keep your tools? Does the order for storing match the way you use them? Could you create a system that you share with your household? How does having this system feel?

3 | LESS STUFF

How do you choose what you need? What tempts you to buy things you don't really need? How might you limit the way advertising leaks into your life and mind?

4 | ONE BY ONE

Can you spot opportunities to take care of the things in your life one by one? Do you own more things than you need? How might you (and your household) free yourself from some of these?

5 | LESS WASTE

Drawing on the ideas of lean manufacturing, can you find ways to group together the jobs you do at home? Notice what happens to how you feel and your free time.

6 | APPRECIATING QUALITY

Consider what quality means to you. How much is about the outer look and how much about the inner workings? Can you find the opportunity to be a conscious consumer of less?

LOST
THE
PLOT

CHAPTER 8

LOST THE PLOT

Grow vegetables in straight lines

Pascal Sharples | Head Chef

Like most people, I have trouble finding the time to really stop and think. Our lives are busy and only seem to get more congested as modern life finds new ways to take up our thoughts and energy. We seem to have got so used to having to constantly multitask, cramming as much as possible into our time, that we forget the importance of having that time to think, process, and reflect. Genuinely focusing on one task seems an almost laughable concept in the 21st century. But when we take the time to focus on one thing, we allow ourselves to organize our thoughts more clearly and calmly.

NATURE'S PACE

Gardening on my allotment (a tiny patch of land for gardening that I rent from the city council) allows me the space I need to reflect. Pace here is not dictated by email, Twitter, or WhatsApp. The allotment has its own speed, set by the seasons and the soil. The peacefulness here is so wholesome and soothing it frees my mind to wander. I feel like I reconnect with who I am. I can also find a new perspective when I am angry, frustrated, or sad. The allotment helps me manage some of the negative emotion I struggle to deal with at home and work.

The connection with nature is important to me, too. The colors are natural. There is stone and wood, and there are lush greens. The textures are softened by wind and rain. I've disconnected from the mainframe and plugged into something more organic. Still connected to the world but in a different way, I slow down to the speed of the patch and truly breathe.

" "

THE SPACE
FREES ME TO
BE <u>CLEAR OF MY</u>
<u>MIND'S WEEDS</u>

SPRING: THE CEREBRAL SEEDBED

Preparing the patch for planting involves clearing the bed of weeds, turning over the earth, and breaking down the lumps of soil. This gives the seeds the best chance of germinating and taking root.

It is much like my thought process when I'm here. The space frees me to be clear of my mind's weeds. Focusing on one simple task allows me to turn over ideas and reflections in my head. Breaking down any frustrations or obstacles makes them much easier to manage. Ideas have the best chance of taking shape and growing into solutions. Did I need to push my point so hard with my colleague? Did I truly listen to my partner and hear what she was really saying? I find answers to these types of question when I allow myself the clarity of mind to work my cerebral seedbed into a fine tilth.

I plant the seeds and seedlings in neat, ordered rows. I like the esthetic feel of the symmetry and structure. It's uncluttered, not immaculate by any means, but there's an order and I own it. This space away from domestic and work life reconnects me to my innermost thoughts and aspirations.

An organic train of thought

The soil and plants need nourishment to flourish. I follow organic principles, using no artificial fertilizers, just natural soil improvers like manure and compost. Forcing crops to grow faster and bigger using inorganic methods results in much poorer-quality produce. It's less tasty and contains much smaller quantities of nutrients.

The same can be said for the best ideas. Grown organically, not rushed or conceived under pressure, our ideas take shape at the right pace and with the right balance of intellectual nourishment. Under these conditions, I start to see how I can manage my emotional well-being more positively and how this adds a lightness and ease to my personal relationships.

SUMMER: WEEDING THE PATCH

Now the seeds have been sown and the plants are starting to grow. Things are not quite that simple, though. Just as the shoots begin to emerge and reach for the light, weeds and pests appear to spoil the party. Reducing competition from weeds means that the plants have the space to fill out and don't have to fight for light and root space. Slugs and snails are gastropods; this literally means "stomach foot." Keeping these pests at bay is vital to prevent seedlings and immature plants from being nibbled to a stump before they have the time to fulfill their potential. To do this successfully I need to tend the patch regularly. Coming in like some sort of herbicidal Blitzkrieg simply won't do. Little and often is the key. This stops the weeds from taking root and makes them easier to remove without disturbing my crops.

"JUST AS THE SHOOTS BEGIN TO EMERGE AND REACH FOR THE LIGHT, WEEDS AND PESTS APPEAR TO SPOIL THE PARTY"

This is analogous to our own development of ideas. Free of our personal weeds, without doubt or negativity, our ideas and creativity reach out to the light and spread their roots unhindered. Tending to them regularly in small amounts reduces the chances of losing the lightness I am starting to find.

The head shed

At the allotment, I have the tools to deal with invading slugs and snails when they rear their heads. A quick hoe here, a beer trap there, and I can keep on top of the threat they pose.

In my life I've struggled to keep personal slugs from interfering with my emotions. I hadn't really confronted until my mid-thirties some deep-rooted, intimate trauma I suffered early in my life. I found it hard to do so at first, because opening old wounds brought back a lot of negative emotions. I was upset and angry. The memories of childhood would leave me on edge at home, and this left my partner and children worrying whether I would snap or shout at seemingly innocuous things. Why couldn't I deal with these feelings without becoming angry?

"   "

GENUINELY FOCUSING ON ONE TASK SEEMS <u>AN ALMOST</u> <u>LAUGHABLE</u> CONCEPT IN THE 21ST CENTURY

To keep on top of those frustrations, I needed to find the right tools—the equivalent of my favorite Dutch hoe and trusty spade in my shed. I resolved to build my own emotional toolshed and fill it with the things I needed to stay happier and more mindful of my personal relationships. Seeking out help and advice on the best tools to use, I started looking at why I dealt with specific situations in the way I did. I realized that I could unintentionally communicate in a self-serving way, so I adjusted the way I communicated with colleagues and my partner to have more constructive, healthier dialogue. I stopped talking as much and started to listen more, almost as if I were pruning my conversations with verbal shears.

Personal pollination
During the summer months the allotment reaches its optimum growing potential. The soil is warm, the sun shines, and the pollinating insects fly freely from flower to flower. Seeing all these elements working in harmony is truly wondrous. It gives me an almost primeval connection to the natural world. The basic elements of raising and tending crops have remained essentially the same for millennia, particularly at this scale, away from the mechanization and the reliance on artificial fertilizers and pest-control methods found in industrial-scale farming.

Many people find this sort of connection to the outdoors important in their lives. Whether it's going out for a jog or a cycle, playing golf, or walking the dog, spending time outside refreshes the mind. It promotes calmness and the means to unwind, which are sometimes lacking in our lives. Work pressures and home-life commitments have steadily chipped away at the time and space we have to think and breathe. I would never have started to deal with my emotional issues without the space afforded me by the allotment.

Irrigation of creativity
The plants grow fast in the hot sun, and they need the right amount of water and nutrients to keep them hydrated and healthy. The simple task of filling up the watering can and pouring its contents onto the soil allows my mind itself to rehydrate and reflect on the progress my own ideas and personal changes are making. I feed my plants to give them the nourishment they require to grow to their potential and provide the best quality and quantity of produce possible.

Here I can ask myself intimate questions. Am I feeding my mind with the right ideas? Am I letting my internal water table run dry and starving myself of the chance to really connect with people? These questions are easier for me to answer honestly when I'm focusing on just one simple task. I know I am truly deep in thought when I feel a cold splash on my feet as I water my shoes instead of the zucchini.

FALL: HARVEST THE FRUITS OF LABOR

One of the first things I crop are potatoes. My sons love digging through the soil to see who can find the hidden treasure. Excited shouts of "Potato!" fill the air. It feels so real and I particularly like seeing the whole plant coming out of the ground. Tubers and roots connect the plant to the soil, and the leaves to the sun and air. The fact that all the genetic information to create entire new plants is stored in seeds and tubers never ceases to amaze me.

I have that potential, too, I realize. My embryonic aspirations have all the DNA they need to grow into something amazing and transform elements of my life that hold me back. I've started to let them grow. I'm improving their conditions and I can see them blossom in front of me. Just as I will now enjoy the fruits of my labor at the dinner table, it's important to enjoy what I am cropping in life. I feel better, and more at peace, by dealing with emotions more healthily. Listening more carefully and communicating with less of a personal agenda means my home and work lives are less stressful and more enjoyable. Taking some time to feel proud of my progress makes the difficult part of my mission—to become a happier, calmer me—more manageable and motivates me to continue my journey.

Sharing moments like these with the boys reminds me of the importance of what I am doing in a happy, energizing way. They are also my plants, needing nurture and the right conditions to grow into happy, well-adjusted young men.

The cabbage patch caper

As the milder months continue we often find ourselves with gluts of fresh fruit and vegetables. There are way more green snap beans than one family can eat, and I always end up growing enough zucchini to put a Tuscan market gardener to shame. This means my less green-fingered friends and neighbors regularly have a plastic bag of green beans left at their door or have an armful of rhubarb passed over the fence. Surplus produce and plants are also swapped and given away on the allotment. If someone's crop of pea shoots gets nibbled, there will usually be another allotmenteer who has some to spare.

"THEY ARE ALSO MY PLANTS, NEEDING NURTURE AND THE RIGHT CONDITIONS TO GROW INTO HAPPY, WELL-ADJUSTED YOUNG MEN"

One particular allotment old hand, Dave, gave me an entire tray of cabbage plants when my first attempt at growing brassicas failed miserably. I was very grateful and told him that I would give him some of the cabbages I managed to grow from his tray. He said that he didn't want anything in return, and I should give any spare cabbages to other people who might use them. It turned out that Dave was a bit of a comic-book aficionado and a big Spiderman fan. Dave told me about a storyline from an old Marvel comic, in which Peter Parker (Spiderman) gives Bruce Banner (The Hulk) his last $5 so he can get a bus out of town. Peter Parker explains that when he was out of luck he had been given $5 by an old man, and this was his way of paying back the debt. This selfless act resonated with Dave and shaped his outlook on giving and receiving.

This got me thinking about my attitude toward giving. I had always considered myself as generous and believed that I put other people first. That was true to a degree but I've come to realize that I would often feel let down if those actions weren't reciprocated in a like-for-like fashion. My generosity could also be a little self-serving in the sense that I would want to be seen to be generous, rather than really considering whether my help or what I was giving was really needed. I was touched by the total selflessness of my allotment companion and resolved to make this part of my way of thinking.

"AM I FEEDING MY MIND WITH THE RIGHT IDEAS?"

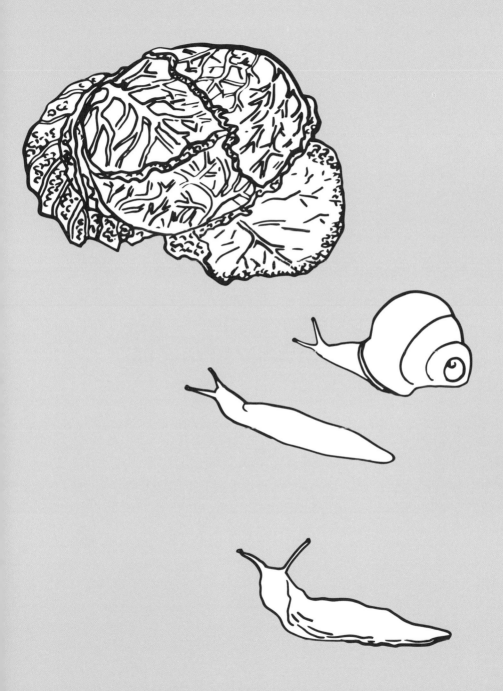

WINTER: GOING TO GROUND

When fall approaches, the patch starts to wind down. The energy of the summer is replaced by shorter, colder days. Plants either come to the end of their life cycle or start to die back, in order to rest and conserve their energy, ready to come alive again next year.

I, too, need to rest my mind and allow my emotional roots to recharge. The changes I've made and the journey I've taken have both been hugely positive but also tiring at times. I sometimes feel like I am mentally running on empty.

"I, TOO, NEED TO REST MY MIND AND ALLOW MY EMOTIONAL ROOTS TO RECHARGE"

I need to make sure that I am not putting too much pressure on myself to make changes. Spending time on the plot gives me somewhere to think, but it also provides a place where I don't need to think if I don't want to. I can just dig, or hoe, or water. No deep reflections or dissection of my psyche, simply pottering around getting lost in the plot.

GET THE PLOT HABIT

Ideas for growing in straight lines

1 | PLANTING

Choose a spot to grow, however small (a windowsill is fine). Prepare the soil. Choose your seeds. Give them space. As you are working the soil, choose an aspiration to focus on during this gardener's year.

2 | WEEDING

Gently tend your young shoots. In the early days, their fragility demands regular care and protection. Spend a little time each day working toward your aspiration. Be kind to yourself, rewarding small growth and making steps easy.

3 | TOOLS

If mini-beasts tamper with your growing plants, seek advice and search for tools fit for the job. As your aspiration takes shape, seek out support through people and resources that will help you navigate over the hurdles.

4 | HYDRATING CREATIVITY

Water your growing shrubs little and often. A drought followed by a deluge can have serious consequences. Consider your aspiration and become aware of the environment and food that results in a leap of growth.

5 | HARVEST FRUITS

Enjoy what you have created as flowers and fruits emerge. Recognize how your aspiration has taken shape. Acknowledge your efforts and be grateful for your findings that led to a new direction.

6 | RESTING EARTH

Clear the soil once the plants have finished their cycle and let it rest untouched for a while. Allow yourself to just be for a time without the need to seek the next aspiration. Create space to rejuvenate.

CHOP, CHOP, CHOP

CHAPTER 9

CHOP, CHOP, CHOP

A more conscious way of cooking

Meredith Whitely | Food at Heart

In our rushed and busy world, many of us are seeking out soothing moments of stillness and reflection. Just type the phrase "finding Zen" into your search engine and you'll get millions of results. As life seems to become more hectic, fractured, and full-on, our craving for Zenlike quiet and focus grows.

126

The origins of Zen lie in the practice of Buddhist monks. It's the Japanese pronunciation of a Chinese strand of Buddhism (Chan Buddhism to be exact), but the word found its way into Western culture, representing a multitude of activities with peaceful connotations. In modern times Zen has become a catchall for many things that are very or vaguely Zen, depending on how liberal the author has been with their interpretation.

However, you don't need to retreat to the mountains, live like a hermit, or lead a monastic life to pursue the need to pause (though, of course, you can also do this if you want to).

We can learn a lot from the approach of Zen Buddhist monks and incorporate some of their perspectives and practices into our daily living (see also Chapter 2). This includes our time in the kitchen. In Zen practice, after sitting *zazen* (sitting meditation), two of the most important meditative and mindful activities are cooking and cleaning. These everyday tasks provide an opportunity to be mindful, when done with a little care, attention, and appreciation. This is something that has been very valuable in my own life.

" "

THERE WAS ALSO A GREAT ACHIEVEMENT AND SATISFACTION CONNECTED TO MAKING SOMETHING WITH MY OWN HANDS

COOKING FIRSTS

For a long time, the kitchen has been my place of reflection and sanctuary. Some of my earliest memories include being at the kitchen worktop with my mother, who was and is a huge influence on my love of food and cooking. I knew from an early age there was something special about this place of creation and creativity.

As an occasionally wild, emotional, and "expressive" child, I liked the focus that cooking brought me. There was also a great achievement and satisfaction connected to making something with my own hands. The anticipation and excitement prompted by delicious smells wafting from the oven never dulled, even if that meant sometimes trying to prise cookies and cakes hot from the baking pans before they were quite ready.

Once I was allowed to get a little involved in the kitchen, from the age of five or so, I particularly loved making butterfly cupcakes, scooping out the center of the baked cupcake to cut it in half and make wings, which were neatly perched on whipped cream or buttercream that filled the hole. Actually, that's a bit of a lie; my very favorite part was licking the spoon or bowl, and as one of five siblings, if I managed to get a decent amount then this was something to be treasured. The wing cutting was a close second.

But the kitchen was about more than making cake. It was a place of refuge where I would sit on the floor with cookbooks and magazines laid out in front of me. I could quite happily while away the time looking at pictures, reading recipes, and planning a cake for my next birthday, even if it was still many months away. It's therefore probably no surprise that in adulthood I still often feel most at home in the kitchen.

Over the years the kitchen has been a source of inspiration in many areas of my life. When I had a difficult problem at work or was feeling emotional or stressed, a bout of breadmaking or cookie creation revived me. I even liked to knead dough in my university study breaks. It was a great way to switch my mind into a different way of thinking; while I was paying attention to the dough, my mind could unconsciously work through other issues.

I was able to tell when I hadn't done any creative cooking for a while: I'd feel myself getting touchy or frustrated, or just a bit flat. There was almost an internal sigh of relief when I opened the cupboards, pulled out my ingredients, and got working.

The importance of this became very apparent to me when I moved into my current house. We didn't have an oven and we survived for a few months cooking on a barbecue with a single gas burner. At first it was fun trying to re-create some dishes in our restricted cooking circumstances, but my hands and heart were itching to create again (and I was craving homemade bread and oven-roasted vegetables).

"I'D FEEL MYSELF GETTING TOUCHY OR FRUSTRATED, OR JUST A BIT FLAT. THERE WAS ALMOST AN INTERNAL SIGH OF RELIEF WHEN I OPENED THE CUPBOARDS, PULLED OUT MY INGREDIENTS, AND GOT WORKING."

Our solution was a $12 oven from eBay to tide us over. It was one of the best purchases I've ever made, for the pure burst of pleasure it provided. Even though the temperature was a little erratic, I could just about bake a cake if I kept an eye on things. Even if it looked like something from a 1970s studio apartment, it did the job until we got something a little better, at which point we handed it over to a new and grateful recipient in similar kitchen circumstances. It felt good to pass this on knowing the new owner would also get cooking joy from an item many others would think of as useless. It's just one very small example among many of the way that food and cooking give us the power to pay forward a little kindness and generosity.

" "

I'D LOVE FOR YOU TO THINK OF YOUR KITCHEN AS A <u>PLACE OF PLAY</u> <u>AND CREATIVITY</u>

TUMMY TROUBLE CALLING...

There was a period when my kitchen became a bit of a battleground with my digestion. As is common for many people in the West, I have suffered, and sometimes still do, from uncomfortable digestive issues. I experience pretty typical symptoms, which range from a swollen and painful belly to sometimes needing to make sure I don't get too far from the bathroom.

At my low point about three years ago, I was able to eat some basic vegetables and white rice, and everything else seemed to cause me digestive upsets. I went through a process of taking foods in and out of my diet to try to analyze what was affecting me the most. This was while consulting various medical specialists to see if they could shed some light on what was happening. I experimented with flavors to make things more interesting, but it was difficult and frustrating for a lover of good food.

What all the medical specialists agreed on was that stress was a major trigger, so regardless of any medical intervention, I needed to learn how to manage this effectively. Up to this point I had tried t'ai chi, Pilates, yoga, occasional meditation, and regular running in an attempt to settle things. Even though they would sometimes ease things a little, there was no significant change as I would still slip into old ways of thinking and busy doing. My digestion became an ever-louder early-warning system that I desperately tried to block out, until eventually I could ignore it no more.

STARTING TO SLOW DOWN

This stomach blip turned out to be a blessing in disguise; it forced me to sit up and pay attention, and to finally listen to what my body was trying to tell me. I also started to truly recognize the need, and beauty, of slowing down. This included a bit of slowing down physically, and doing this more consistently, but also involved the way I cooked and ate. My desire for busy complexity was replaced by a need for simplicity and slowness, which included consuming fewer ingredients in dishes to be gentle on my digestion, and preparing them in dishes slowly and considerately. I started to rediscover genuine pleasure in these simple ingredients. I also started to learn to go with my stomach, instead of trying to fight against it.

This experience guided me toward a much deeper consideration of the senses, and an understanding of how to involve them more consciously in cooking and tasting. It ultimately led me down the path of creating my business, Food at Heart. I wanted to help other people experience the pleasure of tasting and exploring the beautiful flavors of everyday foods. By approaching cooking and eating with a positive and open mind-set and a little focus, we can nourish ourselves physically and emotionally.

COMING TO YOUR SENSES

How can you use your senses in the kitchen? Here are just a few suggestions to get you started:

Sight

We do indeed eat with our eyes. Color can determine our perception of taste, sometimes overriding other senses. This was shown in a famous study at the University of Bordeaux in which wine-science students unwittingly assigned "red wine" tasting notes to a white wine that had been dyed with a flavorless dye.

But color goes beyond this; it's a beautiful way to add a little happiness to your cooking. Lots of color means lots of variety, which is a good thing, but who can deny the pleasure of a streak of frozen red berries through your porridge on a gray morning, or a splash of vivid green spinach in a warming curry?

Filling your kitchen with vibrant and inspiring colors excites your eyes and taste buds. From seasonal vegetables and fruits to a small selection of spices, there are plenty of ways you can get color into your fridge and cupboards. Move away from beige and think of creative ways to add rainbows to your food.

Sound

Crunch, crackle, sizzle, pop, whack: our kitchen is full of sounds. I sometimes get into an almost meditative rhythm with the chop, chop, chop of a knife. Listen carefully to the sounds your food makes on the cutting board, in the skillet, and in your mouth. Our ears are pretty smart. A fun experiment to try is to see if you, like most people, can tell, just through listening, the difference between coffee and water being poured.

For a full aural treat, pop a pot of popcorn. Listen carefully as the kernels start to pop in their covered pot, slowly at first, then firing off in rapid explosions, before slowing to a canter, and dawdle. You'll know they are then ready to eat, covered in a little silky butter and flakes of sea salt. They'll crunch and pop all over again, but this time in your mouth.

"EVEN AS AN ADULT IT'S LOVELY TO SQUISH SOMETHING SOFT THROUGH YOUR FINGERS"

Touch

As I discovered in my early breadmaking days, touch is a powerful way to connect with ingredients, so don't be squeamish about getting your hands in there. I use my hands to bring together cookie dough, to dress salads, to squeeze the juice out of lemons, and to separate egg yolks from their viscous, runny whites. Think of it as a chance to be playful. Even as an adult it's lovely to squish something soft through your fingers.

Best of all is kneading dough. Over time you start to get to know by touch when it has reached the springiness you want, as you feel the mixture move from sticky and claggy to smooth and elastic. The rhythmic movement back and forth over the kitchen counter is a beautiful antidote to a day of hurry.

Smell

Smell is one of our most important senses when it comes to taste. A lot of what we call taste, and our perception of flavor, is down to smell. We have two types of smell: orthonasal (nose smelling) and retronasal (mouth smelling). The second type happens when we chew our food and breathe out, pushing odors back up our throat. This is why it's so important to remember to pay attention to breathing when you're in the kitchen.

Make the most of this by freshly crushing spices whenever possible, including lots of black pepper, and breathing in their aroma. Or lean over a gently frying mixture of onion and garlic, and inhale. Or bake something full of cardamom or

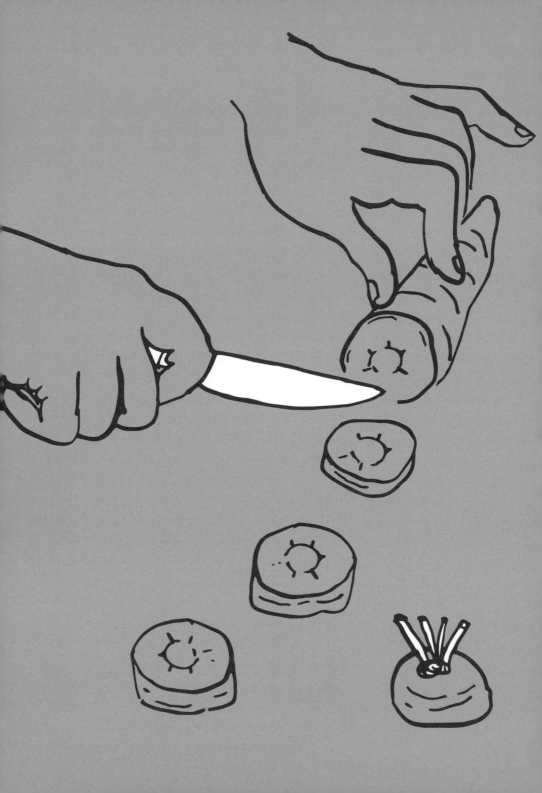

"GET INTO A MEDITATIVE RHYTHM WITH THE CHOP, CHOP, CHOP OF A KNIFE"

" "

THIS IS A JOURNEY THAT NEVER REALLY ENDS AND ALWAYS <u>REVEALS</u> <u>A SLIGHTLY NEW</u> <u>LAYER AND TASTE</u>

ginger (or both!) and stand by the oven as they cook to let the spicy fragrance wash over you.

One of the best ingredients to smell deeply, both in your nose and mouth, is good-quality dark chocolate. With hundreds of flavor compounds, even more than red wine, chocolate is an ingredient that continues to delight me. Trying the same type of chocolate at different times and on different days reveals whole new levels of aroma.

Taste

The taste of chocolate is particularly affected by what else you've eaten during the day or just beforehand; even just having a cup of coffee affects your palate. Chocolate can also taste a little different if it's eaten at a different temperature as the day gets warmer, or if you chew your chocolate instead of letting it melt in your mouth. I even find that the mood I'm in can affect my sense of taste. But you'll only experience this for yourself if you take the time to notice.

I like to taste as I go along while cooking, rather than waiting for a big reveal or strictly following recipes without checking. Take small, focused mouthfuls and pay attention to the flavors you detect. Do you need a sprinkle more of this and a dash of that? Layer flavors and tastes gently and with care. A heavy hand can lead to oversalting or imbalance. Think about sweet, salty, sour, bitter, and umami tastes, and how you can get them working in harmony.

PLAYING IN THE KITCHEN

This might all sound a bit serious, but I'd love for you to think of your kitchen as a place of play and creativity. It's possible to be focused and have fun at the same time—fortunately the two things don't have to be mutually exclusive.

Maybe you'd like to try out different ingredients, cook a new recipe, or experiment with an unfamiliar kitchen tool to keep things fresh. You could try tasting something you've eaten many times, but with a new flavor or seasoning added. I love playing around with flavors and exploring which goes with what.

This leads me back to chocolate again (something that often happens in my kitchen). Good-quality chocolate is one of my favorite ingredients to cook with. Flavors can range from smoky to sweet, and from earthy to grassy, depending on the type of chocolate and where it's from.

It's also one of the best foods through which to start understanding the benefits of more focused tasting. When you taste good chocolate slowly, letting it melt in your mouth rather than chewing it, it releases a whole array of aromas; the longer these remain in your mouth, the more they develop. Like perfume, with its base, middle, and top notes, chocolate has different stages of flavor that flow up and down, in and out.

Line up a few small pieces of different types of chocolate to taste, considering the aroma, flavor, mouthfeel, and texture. It's the starting point for identifying other flavors that might match. One of my current favorites is dark chocolate with dried apricot, rosemary, and ginger, but I've also been known to nibble thoughtfully on a delicious mixture of rich Ecuadorian dark chocolate and slivers of black olives. The only things I draw the line at for pairing with chocolate are raw onion and raw garlic; everything else is fair game.

This is where the importance of paying attention comes into play. Focus is needed to taste and listen and match—and then repeat the whole process again. This is a journey that never really ends and always reveals a slightly new layer and taste. If there's ever been a time in the kitchen when I've approached anything approximating Zenlike focus, it has involved chocolate.

By taking a note out of the Zen Buddhist book, you too can use the time in your kitchen as an opportunity to pay attention. Cooking is a time to celebrate a connection with food and ingredients, using all the senses. If you approach your kitchen and cooking with curiosity and wonder, you might be surprised at what you discover. Instead of using it as a time to switch off, you can instead switch on.

GET THE CHOP CHOP HABIT

Ideas for conscious cooking

1 | SIMPLICITY

Enjoy the pleasure of preparing food. It doesn't need to be complicated; there is beauty and gratitude in celebrating simple, seasonal ingredients and making the most of what you have.

2 | CONSIDERED CONSUMPTION

Try applying a more minimalist approach to your kitchen by not buying too much in the first place, so you don't end up with redundant spices or a pasta machine gathering dust in the cupboard. Buy what you need, enjoy, and will use, and give away anything you don't.

3 | SLOW EATING

Instead of chomping quickly, slow down, eat small mouthfuls, and breathe. Enjoy the aromas, sounds, and feel of your kitchen endeavors.

4 | SLOW COOKING

If possible, avoid being a whirling kitchen dervish, flinging things around with wild abandon. Be expressive, but give yourself a little time to stir your pot and pause.

5 | LOVING FOOD

Fill your kitchen with aromas and ingredients that make *you* happy. Eat a wider range of real, seasonal foods and explore lots of flavors. Choosing and creating food with love also gives you an opportunity to offer this love on to other mouths you feed.

6 | YOUR RULES

Don't let ideas of what you "should" be eating rule your kitchen. Let your body, mouth, and senses guide you instead. And if you reach a state of Zen enlightenment, well, that's fantastic, too!

MEANINGFUL MESSAROUND

CHAPTER 10

CHAPTER 10

MEANINGFUL MESSAROUND

Do you want to play with me?

Annabelle van Nieuwkoop-Read | Dramatherapist

I am crawling around on the floor being what I hope is a lion. My knees hurt and I regret yet again that I chose to wear a skirt to work. I do not have a good-enough roar; no it's still is not a good-enough roar. I resist swearing. Oh, I have to be a rabbit, do I? I resist swearing. I have to hop as fast as a rabbit around the room? I resist swearing out loud. I am not hopping high enough? I swear in a whisper. I will give you high enough! I put all my energy into the highest bunny jump anyone has ever mastered. I am serious about this bunny hop. I am going to ace this hop! Here I go...yes, I have got this hop *going on*...and, whack, I am on the floor, skirt over my head, and the giggles begin.

I realize I am still lying on the floor and I look up to see a giggling five-year-old named Sam looking down on me. Sam takes a moment to ponder the situation; in fact, he takes more than a moment. He takes it all in and it feels like he is looking down on me for hours. He asks with curious eyes:

"Annabelle, are you an adult or a child?"

I laugh harder and I cannot help myself. I love the idea that Sam believes I could be a child. He is intelligent enough to know that physically I am not a child but it makes me happy to know that he has entered into a playful experience with me that enables us to escape reality for a while. To Sam I was a lion, I was a rabbit, and I was someone who was free and enjoying the experience of play.

" "

SCREENS

ARE EVERYWHERE,
IN EVERY HOUSE,
IN EVERY ROOM
AND IN EVERY HAND

SCREENS

Every Monday for the past 11 years I have been playing in a tiny designated room (almost a closet). In this room I play the role of a play therapist. I help children who feel disconnected to the world to reconnect to it through the art of play. Sometimes I feel the fact that these children do not play in their everyday life is the very reason that they are so disconnected from the world.

Outside play, role play, and family board games have been replaced by screens. Screens are everywhere, in every house, in every room, and in every hand. I sometimes wonder, if aliens did exist and were to come and visit us, whether people would even notice, because they wouldn't be looking up to see what was going on around them anyway. Screens stop us from playing with our children, they stop our children from playing with our children, they stop us from playing with us and screens…well, screens just stop us from seeing one another and existing together in the moment. They stop us from playing.

LET YOUR CHILD BE FREE

Recently while browsing through an in-flight magazine I was perplexed by a GPS tracking system offered for children. Don't get me wrong, there is part of me that loves the idea of knowing exactly where my seven-year-old is at all times. She is a wild spirit and, when given the chance to explore, she does. I have had endless heart-stopping moments when I have not known exactly which house on our street she is in, what tree she is hanging from, or what mud pool she is diving into. What if she did have a tracking system? I wouldn't have to ever worry again, right?

Wrong.

I know my daughter is out there pushing boundaries, I know she is going that bit further past the post I told her not to, I know she is pulling that bit harder on the tree branch that I told her to leave alone, I know she is knocking on the neighbors' door and running away, and I am okay with it. I am okay with it because she is playing, she is being a child. Not only is she playing but also she is learning. She is learning to take risks and the consequences of them. She is learning to create her own boundaries, and she is learning to be alone, to get bored, and to seek out connections to relieve that boredom. It is hard to let her go and I resist the urge to know where she is every moment of the day, but I remind myself that she is not attached to a screen, and all the resistance I feel is worth it.

GROWING THROUGH RISKS

I am that mother who sits on the bench in the park just out of my children's vision. I know that they are pushing one another off the swing because the other one believes they got there first. I am not running to them to solve their conflict because I believe they can solve it themselves. What if they don't? Well, I will hear it if they don't, and if I don't hear it, then one of them will make sure I do hear it. (Apart from that, I am enjoying some much-needed screen time and catching up on how many likes my latest social media post got—oops, you got me.) I need my time as much as they need theirs and I am not ashamed of it.

> ## "SHE IS LEARNING TO CREATE HER OWN BOUNDARIES, AND SHE IS LEARNING TO BE ALONE, TO GET BORED, AND TO SEEK OUT CONNECTIONS"

I am that mother who lets her children fall and does not run to them. Yes, I let them fall, you read that right and, yes, you also read it right that I do not run to them. Yes, I feel sorry for them when it happens and, yes, they feel sorry for themselves. I take a mindful moment. What is a mindful moment? It is basically a moment to consider if the scream from the child is an "I have broken my arm" scream or if it is an "I am pretending I have broken my arm in order to get an ice cream from Mommy who will feel sorry for me" scream. After my mindful moment they have either given up and started playing again or they are still lying there, and by this point either a running mommy has taken over or I have the look of shame of the running mommy as she arrives on the scene a little later than she expected.

" "

I ALSO WANT TO
PROTECT THEM FROM
WHAT COMES WITH A
LIFE OF SCREEN TIME,
INSIDE TIME, AND
OVERPROTECTION-BY-
PARENTS TIME

I am that mother who lets her children hang from high heights without hovering under them to be there in case they fall. Again, here is the time for one of those mindful moments. I can see my child hanging from the edge of a playground climbing frame. I can see that they need to somehow make their way from that height to the ground. One small move could mean a broken arm and, as mindful as I am, I hate sitting in after-hours doctor's waiting rooms. I resist the urge to hover under my child, and the mindful moment has passed. I have let them fall and, after letting them fall alone, there will be many moments when they stop falling and they realize they landed on two feet from a great height and they did it alone. The joy!

Are you resisting letting your child play outside alone? Are you resisting letting them fall? Are you resisting the urge to be a hovering parent? I get it, since I feel it, too. I want to protect my children from everything out there, but I also want to protect them from what comes with a life of screen time, inside time, and overprotection-by-parents time. Take a few steps back; the higher your internal resistance, the slower and smaller the steps you should take. You can do it!

LET THE INNER CHILD IN *YOU* BE FREE

If we know it is so important to let our children play freely and we can see how this helps them connect to the world, why do we stop playing as adults? At some point between childhood and adulthood, we **cease** playing, and it appears that we live in a society of all work and no play.

I have to confess that I don't feel this way myself. Don't get me wrong. There have been periods in my life when that wasn't the case. I have been in that mundane groove of work, driving the kids to school, dinner, collapse on couch, sleep, and repeat. When in this rut, I am crying out from inside that I want out! I want to play! Yes, I want to play as an adult, not play for work but play for me! I have to spend most of my working days being an adult and pretending to be serious. After a day of long meetings that are sometimes about really difficult and emotional subjects, I reach breaking point. The inner child in me has been knocking from the inside all day. I just can't take life that seriously for long periods of time. I can't take myself that seriously. Yes, I love emotional depth in relationships but I also love to have fun, dance, be uncouth, be silly, and giggle.

ADULT PLAYTIME

Maybe taking the leap into adult play feels just like that—a huge leap out of our comfort zone. Just as it's essential for kids, I think it is for adults, too. The question is, how do we do it?

When children play they experiment with life. This experimenting through acting out possible outcomes gives a way to explore possibilities, test boundaries, try out new skills, and tell stories. As adults we still need to do all of these things but sometimes our day-to-day lives offer less opportunity for this. When we play together, we build bonds with one another. We form partners who, through play, agree to be our allies in the playful exploration of the possible. Sometimes finding a first step, a small way in can be more palatable than being invited to attend a more radical "play event." Adult play doesn't need to be adults crawling around pretending to be lions. Think of leaders who interweave playful ideas and games into how they run groups, giving license to innovate. Friends you may have who broach tough topics of conversation with a lightness and presence that makes sharing with them easy are often being playful in their approach.

So, is it okay for a 35-year-old married mother of two to approach a male colleague and ask him, "Do you want to play with me some time?" I am forever having these playful interactions that I like to call "Bridget Jones moments." As the words fall out of my mouth, I can hear a chorus of laughter and snickers, because this clearly is misinterpreted as, "Would you like to jump into bed with me and be playful?" Can anyone ever ask another adult, "Do you want to play with me some time?" without the other feeling sexually harassed or as if they are being undressed in one sweeping look?

Why do the words "adult" and "play" immediately make us think of sex? At what point does the innocence of playing together as a child turn into flirting as teenagers? Can we engage in something as emotive and connected as play with other adults while feeling comfortable that we can maintain our sexual boundaries? I work in a high school for three days a week, so teenagers flirting, playing with managing these boundaries, is something I get to see on a regular basis. Teenagers tend to flirt in very awkward ways. A 13-year-old boy finds a girl attractive, so he throws something in her face to get her attention.

The girl is, of course, not amused by the object that gets thrown in her face, and the boy looks on embarrassed as he realizes he has just done the most awkward thing ever. Girls throw their hair around in all directions and squeal in high-pitched voices; again, this doesn't seem to gain the attention they are seeking. At around the age of 16, the teenage flirting takes a step up the flirt ladder. They seem to have got the "gentle touch on the shoulder" thing going on by this age. In all of these interactions there is a lot of giggling, fun, joking, and mockery. It is playful.

So at some point in adulthood we decide to stop flirting, to settle down, and to end the play.

"WHY DO THE WORDS 'ADULT' AND 'PLAY' IMMEDIATELY MAKE US THINK OF SEX?"

It feels as though there is a little of that teenage fear of being misunderstood or made to look foolish that sticks with us and maybe even grows in adulthood. Can we learn to resist this fear? When I have done this myself I am amazed at how quickly others often join in. The dance floor at a party, wedding, or even nightclub is the perfect example. Within reason, if you stride out and start dancing as if no-one is watching, the mood you create often begins to spread, others join in, move a little more freely, smile a little more readily, and become part of a group dance play session. Maybe it's easier when language doesn't get in the way?

The concept of mindful play really helps with overcoming this resistance and breaking a few taboos. At the heart of mindful play is the idea that we are totally absorbed in the play, free of judgment about ourselves and others, just happily noticing the details and acting on our instincts. If you are in a public place doing this then the total absorption in the activity means you simply don't notice the reaction of other outside observers. This happened recently when I was out with my daughter in a country park. This place is famous for royals of a bygone era having come here to play and to mark this memory there is a

"STRIDE OUT AND START DANCING AS IF NO-ONE IS WATCHING"

little house filled with Victorian toys for visiting children to use. My daughter wanted to dress as a knight and sword fight on the green outside the house with me. I hesitated for a moment but then threw myself into the game with fully absorbed gusto. Within ten minutes three other families had followed suit and adults and children were having a wonderful time as wooden blades clonked and battles cries resounded. I totally believe that seeking out these moments to role-model play is infectious for adults because most people yearn, somewhere deep inside, to play again.

"SEEKING OUT THESE MOMENTS TO ROLE-MODEL PLAY IS INFECTIOUS"

Does adulthood mean that's it then?

Game over?

Noooooo! It really does not need to end here. The game can carry on. Hit the replay button and follow the tips but, most of all, don't think. Just play and enjoy!

GET THE PLAYFUL HABIT

Ideas for inviting meaningful messaround

1 | DAILY PLAY
Give yourself permission to play every day. Try turning the music up, dancing, and singing like you are the best thing ever!

2 | SILLY DAYS
Don't take yourself or your colleagues seriously for an entire day. Add some humor to lunch breaks. Joke, have fun, and share laughter with one another.

3 | KIDS' PLAY
Do you have kids? Incorporate 15 minutes' uninterrupted child-led play into every day. Get down on the floor—make those knees hurt! The child leads and the adult follows. No screens allowed! You don't have kids? Borrow them.

4 | JUST COLOR
There are so many adult coloring books out there but all you really need is paper and pens. Just make shapes and draw what you feel like. Nothing is right or wrong.

5 | GAMES NIGHT
Have one night a week where no screens are allowed. Make this a board-game night with your partner (and older children). Or host a games night with friends or colleagues.

6 | JUST MOVE!
Take up physical activity. You can run, cycle, box, skip, do anything. Just get your heart pumping and let your body move!

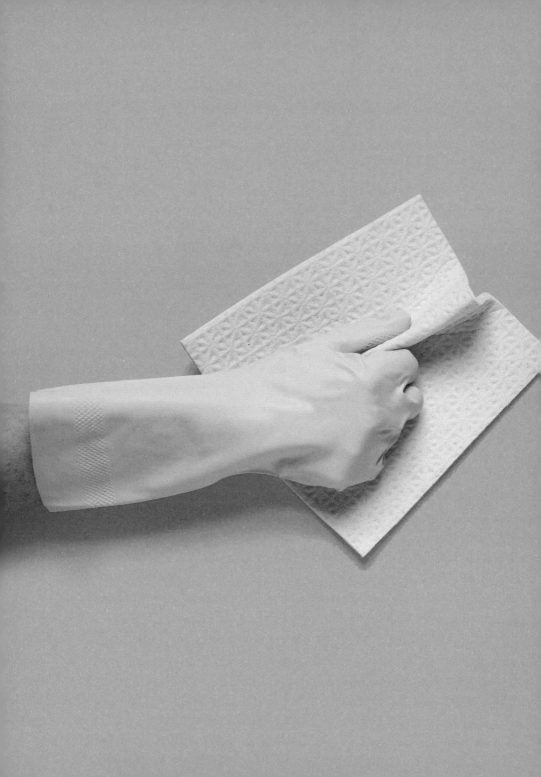

REFERENCES,
RESOURCES
& CREDITS

REFERENCES

Chapter 1

Hanh, Thich Nhat (2008) *The Miracle Of Mindfulness: The Classic Guide to Meditation by the World's Most Revered Master.* London, Rider Publishing

Redzepi, René (March 1, 2017) 'Noma Dishwasher Becomes Co-owner of World-famous Danish Restaurant. *The Guardian online.* www.theguardian.com/lifeandstyle/2017/mar/01/noma-dishwasher-becomes-co-owner-of-world-famous-danish-restaurant

Chapter 2

BBC News (April 9, 2008) 'Cleaning improves mental health'. news.bbc.co.uk/1/hi/health/7338644.stm

Brown, Simon, G. (2009) *The Feng Shui Bible.* London, Octopus Publishing Group Ltd

Coltrane, Scott (2000) 'Research on Household Labor: Modeling and Measuring the Social Embeddedness of Routine Family Work.' In: *Journal of Marriage and Family,* 62(4), 1208–33

Geary, David C. (2004) *The Origin of Mind: Evolution of Brain, Cognition, and General Intelligence.* Washington, American Psychological Association

Jaffe, Eric (April 2, 2017) 'Why Wait? The Science Behind Procrastination.' *Association for Psychological Science online,* www.psychologicalscience.org/observer/why-wait-the-science-behind-procrastination#.WQH014WcHSF

Chapter 4

Dunning, G B. (1971) 'Research in Nonverbal Communication.' In: *Journal of Theory into Practice,* 10(4), 250–8

Leonard, Kelly and Yorton, Tom (2015) *Yes, And: How Improvisation Reverses 'No, But' Thinking and Improves Creativity and Collaboration—Lessons from the Second City.* New York, HarperCollins Publishers

Chapter 5

Jessen, Lauren (March 3, 2017) 'The Benefits of a Gratitude Journal and How to Maintain One.' *The Huffington Post online.* www.huffingtonpost.com/lauren-jessen/gratitude-journal_b_7745854.html

Seligman, Martin (2012) *Flourish.* Melbourne, Australia, Random House

Seligman, Martin (2011) *Learned Optimism.* Melbourne, Australia, Random House

Chapter 6

Nepo, Mark (2000) *The Book of Awakening: Having the Life You Want by Being Present to the Life You Have.* Boston, Conari Press

Chapter 7

Liker, Jeffrey K. (2004) *The Toyota Way: 14 Management Principles from the World's Greatest Manufacturer.* New York, McGraw-Hill Books

Pirsig, Robert (1974) *Zen and the Art of Motorcycle Maintenance*. London, The Bodley Head

Chapter 9
Sheng Yen (2006) *Attaining the Way: A Guide to the Practice of Chan Buddhism*. Boston, Shambhala Publications Inc.

Velden, Dana (2015) *Finding Yourself in the Kitchen*. New York, Rodale Inc.

Chapter 10
Race, Kristen (2014) *Mindful Parenting*. New York, St. Martin's Griffin

RESOURCES
Websites
A great source of information about Martin Seligman's work (see also Chapter 5, page 74) and a free robust questionnaire for exploring your strengths.
www.viacharacter.org

A wonderful organization concerned with enabling people to be happier.
www.actionforhappiness.org

The brain's concept of time and how to stop self-sabotage (see also Chapter 2, page 33).
sepitajima.com/how-to-stop-self-sabotage-by-understanding-your-3-brains/

Take part in the 30-day photo challenge on Facebook.
www.facebook.com/30-day-photo-challenge-133809673351565

Information and an invitation to take part in a regular break from technology.
www.sabbathmanifesto.org

Discover more about the joys and benefits of riding a fixed-gear bicycle (see also Chapter 7, page 100).
www.bikeradar.com/gear/article/riding-a-fixie-will-make-you-a-better-cyclist-18458

Useful resources to help with mindful living and mindful play.
www.mindful.org

An international Buddhist organization that offers a form of teaching readily understandable to a Western audience (see also Chapters 2 and 9, pages 31 and 138). *www.thebuddhistcentre.com*

A deeper dive into applying lean manufacturing principles to everyday living (see also Chapter 7, page 104). *blog.minitab.com/blog/real-world-quality-improvement/everyday-lean-tips-and-tricks-to-use-at-home*

Ideas and current news about being a little more self-sufficient in an urban environment. *www.selfsufficientish.com*

Explanations and an easy how-to guide on making your own keyhole garden (see also Chapter 8). *www.sendacow.org.uk/lessonsfromafrica/resources/keyhole-gardens*

Books

Cohen, Lawrence J. (2012) *Playful Parenting*. New York, Random House USA Inc.

Germer, Christopher K. (2009) *The Mindful Path to Self-Compassion*. New York, The Guilford Press

Murray, Lorraine E. (2012) *Calm Kids: Help Children Relax with Mindful Activities*. Edinburgh, Floris Books

Neff, Kristin (2011) *Self Compassion: Stop Beating Yourself Up and Leave Insecurity Behind*. London, Hodder & Stoughton

Wax, Ruby (2016) *A Mindfulness Guide for the Frazzled*. London, Penguin

Williams, Mark and Penman, Danny (2011) *Mindfulness: A Practical Guide to Finding Peace in a Frantic World*. London, Piatkus

CREDITS

Huge thanks to our talented and insightful authors, artists, and designers whose grit, humor, and passion have made the creation of this book a joy:

Meredith Whitely—*foodatheart.co.uk*
Meredith founded Food at Heart to offer people space to develop a more conscious way of eating and living.

Antonia Thompson—*www.antoniathompson.uk*
Brighton-based artist with a media background (former editor at The Huffington Post, AOL, Sky, and ITV).

John-Paul Flintoff—*www.flintoff.org and www.speaklisten.co.uk*
Writer, performer, and coach who helps organizations and individuals change the world, one conversation at a time.

Ruth Williams—*www.deptstoreforthemind.com*
Business psychologist and director at Department Store for the Mind.

Kate Peers—*madabouttheboys.net*
Writer, frequent contributor to Metro online, and published author in *The Mother Book* by Selfish Mother.

Clare Barry—*www.urbancuriosity.org*
Founder of Urban Curiosity, a wellness and creativity company that helps busy people slow down and see things differently.

Pascal Sharples—Head chef, dad of two, and avid allotmenteer with a passion for growing fresh, natural ingredients to create family feasts.

Annabelle van Nieuwkoop-Read—*www.aread.typepad.com*
English-born dramatherapist based in The Netherlands, specializing in autism. She never really stops playing.

Photography: James Champion—*jch.format.com*
London-based lifestyle and fashion photographer, dedicated to creativity and his cat, Bob.

Illustration: Veronica Wood—*www.veronicawood.co.uk*
Illustrator whose best friends are her bottle of ink and a dip pen. Touching honesty and raw emotion shine through her illustration.

Design: Supafrank Design—*www.supafrank.com*
Katie Steel and Jo Raynsford at Supafrank dig deep enough to unearth the spark, hook, or story, weaving this through their work with expert subtlety.

159